SISYPHUS AND REILLY

Peter Luke

SISYPHUS
AND REILLY

ANDRE DEUTSCH

First published 1972 by
André Deutsch Limited
105 Great Russell Street London WC1

Copyright © 1972 by Peter Luke
All rights reserved

Printed in Great Britain
by Ebenezer Baylis and Son Ltd
The Trinity Press, Worcester, and London

ISBN 233 96351 0

For my children,
Harry, Giana, Anthony,
Anna, Ormódy, Rosario, and Oonagh
to whom this story
is news

'Life, life, life! . . . Aesthetics
is knitting.'

HENRI CARTIER-BRESSON
Paris, November 1962

PROLOGUE

'There should always be some foundation of fact for the most airy fabric, and pure invention is but the talent of a liar,' wrote Lord Byron to John Murray in 1817; and I quote it as a hint to the reader that my somewhat airy fabric is not just pure invention. But those who know something of the circumstances around which this book is written will certainly say at some point that such-and-such a circumstance was not as I have described it, or even that something that I have written is not quite true. There may even be those who having caught me out in some minor inaccuracy or in the bending of a fact will condemn the whole opus as a pack of lies. To them I would quote Livy, who said that he would have made Pompey win the battle of Pharsalia if the turn of the sentence had required it.

At one point in my life I was employed in the drama department of a television company as a staff writer and story editor. In the latter capacity I had an expense account for the purpose of entertaining playwrights or would-be playwrights. One day, having submitted my expenses for a given period to the administrative office, I received a curt note saying, 'What is this piece of fiction?' I replied, 'I am employed here to write fiction.' I was then constrained to departmentalize my writing activities – all a lot of nonsense, of course, but it made me reflect a little on the nature of truth. Rather than try to define it here myself, however, I prefer to quote Lytton Strachey who says, 'Uninterpreted truth is as useless as buried gold; and art is the great interpreter. It alone can unify a vast multitude of facts into a significant whole. . . .'

What, therefore, I have attempted to do in this book, irrespective of historical accuracy, is to use 'my art and sullen craft' as well as I am able in order to make some sense out of the insignificant events that compose the pattern of my life.

P.L.

ACKNOWLEDGMENTS

My thanks are due to Mr Cyril Connolly and to the *Sunday Times* for permission to quote from Mr Connolly's review of *Casanova* by J. Rives Childs. I am grateful to the *Cornhill Magazine* for allowing me to publish in a slightly different form my article entitled 'Te Deum'. The Dolphin Book Company Ltd, have kindly permitted me to quote a quatrain from a poem by Josep Carner, translated into English by Pearse Hutchinson. For permission to reproduce the quotations from *Collected Poems* by Oliver St John Gogarty, I am indebted to Messrs Constable & Co Ltd. To all the above my thanks.

My acknowledgments are due to Messrs Chappell & Co Ltd, for permission to quote from the lyric 'Love Walked in', Copyright 1938 by Gershwin Publishing Corp, words reprinted by permission of Chappell & Co Ltd; 'That Lovely Weekend', copyright 1941 by Messrs Bradbury Wood Ltd, words reprinted by permission; to Messrs Campbell Connelly & Co Ltd and the Dash Music Co Ltd for 'We'll Meet Again'; for 'A Nightingale Sang in Berkeley Square', copyright MCMXL by the Peter Maurice Music Co Ltd. Sole selling agent for USA & Canada, Shapiro, Bernstein & Co Inc. Used by permission; and to K.P.M. Music Group for their permission granted within the British and Commonwealth territory; and to Messrs B. Feldmen & Co Ltd, for 'The White Cliffs of Dover', copyright MCMXL by Shapiro, Bernstein & Co Inc, 666 Fifth Avenue, New York, NY 10019.

I would like to take this opportunity to apologize to my old friend, Sydney Newman, Chairman of the Canadian National Film Board, for presenting him here, albeit affectionately, in caricature rather than in portrait. My fond thanks also go to my brother, and brother Rifleman, Michael Luke, for his criticism of the war-time aspects of the text and, in particular, for allowing me to lift one of his by no means rare *bon mots*. To Diana Athill and Campbell Black my sincere gratitude for their many helpful editorial suggestions. Finally I wish to thank my wife, better known as June Tobin, for her astonishing ability to remember all the words of a great number of war-time songs, despite the fact that she was little more than a child at that time.

P.L.

PART ONE

A*

I

Spero meliora. . . . . Here I am, a not-so-young man with a dry mouth lying full length on a bunk in front of a stove. It is early afternoon at Winter Solstice with the blackbird in the garden making its nightfall noises as the four-o'clock darkness descends on London.

Spero meliora. That is our family motto which being construed means 'I Hope for Better Things'. And I think it was no accident that the Lukach family brought that rallying-cry with them from Hungary when they had to leave in a hurry.

My great-great-grandfather, a Protestant, supported the liberal patriot Lajos Kossuth in the Hungarian War of Independence of 1848–49. As students of modern history will recall, this rebellion, unlike that of Garibaldi in Italy a few years later, failed, and the Kossuthites had to leave their native land or suffer the consequences. My great-great-grandparents fled to the United States, bringing with them little more than the motto.

The Lukach clan were Magyars known to be living in the north of Hungary in the thirteenth century at which time, so I have been told, they occupied themselves in the horse-coping trade. Another school of thought has it that they were also engaged in the cattle-duffing business, which is after all only a side-line of the same activity. However, at this distance of time their pursuits, if not their origins, are more in the nature of legend, or perhaps even myth.

In modern times the most distinguished member of the family to be born in Hungary was my great-great-uncle Vilmos Ormódy, or – to put it the native way – Ormódy Vilmos, a very decent old fellow, whom I remember meeting at Sacher's Hotel in Vienna when I was about twelve years old. Uncle Ormódy was a member of what was then the Felsöház, or Upper House, and I have a photograph of him dressed for a state occasion, his hand resting on a curving sabre, in a uniform – if the word uniform can be applied to a *tenue* of lace and gold, fur and frogging, the whole surmounted by an egret plume – of Ruritanian magnificence.

My grandfather, Joe Lukach, was born in Detroit but came to Europe as a young man where he did well, and perhaps thinking he might do worse, took out British nationality. He married a Viennese Catholic called Eugénie Zamarski.[1] In due course my father was born in London, was educated at Eton and Trinity College, Oxford, and became an English gentleman, a fact that nobody who ever knew Harry Luke senior would deny, but it takes a good Hungarian to bring it off!

And so here am I more than half a century later, another Lukach – or rather, Luke – and, like my forebears at the time they left Hungary, with no more assets in the world but the family motto, *Spero meliora*. Thank God I am an optimist or it would not be much use to me.

Daylight has almost gone and my only light comes from an old-fashioned studio stove which glows away, unaware that I have no money left for another load of fuel. It is a pretty piece of still life with a long black pipe which gets hot all the way up to the roof, thereby heating my bedroom in the gallery as well. I am fond of this stove but I do not pretend that it is in any way conscious of my affection, nor does it respond to the name, 'Bontesse', embossed upon it by the makers. In fact it is a wanton and greedy thing in constant need of care and attention.

The bunk on which I am lying was built for an ancestor on my mother's side, a Fremlin, who was Agent at the court of the Great Mogul in the seventeenth century. It is made of oak and latticework and has two ring-bolts either end for lashing it down at sea. I lie on my elbow being hypnotized by the unwinking, undulating, stare of the stove and, in order to counteract the soporific effect of its warm gaze. I think – or try to think – about money, or rather, the lack of it and the disastrous effect this lack is likely to have on all concerned.

Who *are* concerned? It might be as well at this stage to glance at the *dramatis personae*: apart from myself, who is of course the hero, or anti-hero, there is the person to whom I am still technically married.

[1] Daughter of the Chevalier de Zamarski, of Polish origin.

I first met Lettice on my return to England from Italy in 1944. She had been working in some secret organization where they employed young ladies of good family on the assumption that they were a better security risk than those not out of the 'top drawer'. (I now doubt the validity of this premise, but that is beside the point.) To me, at that time, she seemed the apotheosis of all that was courageous and beautiful in a country hard hit by war. Though, to be fair to myself, I should mention that I had been abroad for nearly three years and Lettice was the first all-white woman I had seen for some time. In any case she was amiable and more or less available and had about her that *noli me tangere* quality that makes some men get excited about nuns and royalty. For my part, the more aloof Lettice was, the more physically attractive I found her. So much the worse for both of us.

I don't suppose Lettice's family were overwhelmed with enthusiasm about our marriage, but they put a good face on it. They were already at that time too old or cold or concerned about their ration books and petrol coupons to raise much objection. Besides I was in a decent regiment then and had shed my blood, though admittedly not in any extravagant quantity, for their country, and these were the sort of things they minded about.

Also concerned, though more indirectly, is my brother Michael. He and I move in rather different circles, though these do intersect here and there: in and out of some Soho pubs and clubs, for instance, and round about the Irish Bohemia of Dublin and Luggala. Michael is nearly six years younger than me which was too wide a gap to allow for close friendship in childhood, however much affection there might have been – and indeed was – between the two of us. Further, for the same reasons, we never overlapped either at school or in the army, though we were at the same schools and in the same regiment. After the war my as-it-were bourgeois marriage must, I think, have aggravated some sense of insecurity in him and for a long time I resented, and took retaliatory measures against, his undeclared war on me and mine. Now I realize my mistake in defending my (then) orthodox position versus his anarchistic one. But, having once

13

been a non-conformist myself, and then being forced into the orthodox camp to which I did not at heart belong, my exasperation grew with every encounter until we could hardly meet without drawing blood. Eventually Lettice barred him the door.

Now that I have achieved at least physical independence from Lettice, Michael's and my relationship is changing for the better. Perhaps our roles will even change in time, with me becoming the anarchist again and he the man in the Savile Row suit. Meanwhile all drastic change is exciting to one's friends whether they be related or not and Michael is gratified to see me jumping ship and striking out for the shore. Of course, he can hardly be expected to see it quite from my point of view, being as I am hull down in deep water and a long way from land.

Next on the cast list must come two boon companions, Louis Le Brocquy and Declan Papadopoulos. One is an Irishman with a Belgian grandfather and the other is Greek with an Irish mother. One, Le Brocquy, is a talented painter, and the other has a variety of talents but none in the sphere of the graphic arts. The former works hard with the talent that he has; the other is forever busy but never works at anything for long. Le Brocquy has an attic studio but hardly ever paints portraits. Papadopoulos owns a portrait of himself but, unlike Dorian Gray, lacks an attic to lock it up in.

Louis' grandfather came to Ireland as a remount officer in the Belgian Army, married there, and founded a line of Irishmen. Ireland's strength has always lain in the fact that she has defeated every invader by the simple expedient of marrying him. By so doing, she has never effectively been conquered. The result of this principle is manifest in Declan who is more Irish than Greek in character. In his case, though, the naturally ꞃʟᴀɪᴄɪúʟᴀᴄ[1] character of the Irish is perhaps underlined by a certain princely indolence perceptible in the Hellenic ethos.

The fifth protagonist in this act of the drama is an elegant female called Frederika who, if she does not exactly have me in thrall, at least has me by the gonads. However, there is no hold in wrestling, so they say, that doesn't have its counter, and there

[1] princely.

14

are many instances in nature where a creature in desperation will leave a limb behind in order to be free.

So much for the principals. For the rest there are Nursemaids, Schoolboys, Beaks, Virgins, Artists, Students, Soldiers, Journalists, Wine Merchants, Distillers, Whores, Scholars, Poets, Priests, Pimps and a whole gallimaufry whom we can safely leave in the green-room while we examine briefly the hero's present predicament.

The first move in my rehabilitation after thirteen years in the wilderness – that is from the day of my demobilization up to the present time – was, as the lawyers with their never failing ability to coin a repulsive phrase put it, 'to desert the matrimonial home'. This was an utterly painful step necessitating the abandonment of my two small and dear children to Lettice and the lawyers. Whether it was a move that will ultimately benefit them remains to be seen, but judging by the Thirty Years War that my parents waged in their matrimonial home 'for the sake of the children', it may well prove to be so. Meanwhile from my point of view the hurt is deep and likely to be permanent.

The second leg of the rehabilitation is a different story altogether; being at once joyful, fearful, purposeful, sensible, irresponsible and inevitable: I have left my job. I have left permanent and pensionable employment with a firm of City wine shippers – for what? I do not know. I am only aware of the urgent necessity to start life again where I left it twenty years ago, and I'm not sure that it can be done.

So here I am in my fortieth year in the deepening twilight of Winter Solstice writing, or thinking about writing, this book.

From time to time a coal within the stove drops with a metallic clink causing the glow temporarily to brighten. These sudden crepitations startle me briefly out of a brown study into which I relapse within seconds.

Then the first shrill of the telephone penetrates deep into my subconscious and rouses my resident guilt. The second ring assaults ganglia in the area of my stomach and brings me to the surface of wakefulness where my eyes open on to the subfusc of a winter afternoon. The third (which, like the third blow of a beating, lands on shock-numbed flesh) activates a conditioned

15

reflex compelling me to answer before it rings another three times. Six rings are the most that Frederika will permit.

Aware of all this, I am also aware that I am not fully awake, that I must cross the room without succumbing to a dizzy spell, that I must pick up the receiver without breathing too heavily, and, finally, that I must instil into my voice an alert matter-of-factness that I am very far from feeling.

To let the instrument ring is an alternative I never now consider. Experiment in lying has always ended painfully. Confronted with failure to answer a call at a time when I am 'known to be in' has, in the past, always led me into a quicksand of untruth which has sometimes been misconstrued – by Frederika – as cover for a real misdemeanour.

Telephone lies as common social currency are a convenience denied me, at least by Frederika. Talking to her on the telephone tends to make me stammer and I have even been known to make false confessions – petty ones like owning up to having had too much to drink the night before – lest by my silence she should suspect me of worse. In my relations with Frederika the telephone has become an auricular peeping-Tom, an asdic by which sound reflexes probe the relatively innocent, but intimate, details of my life.

The bell ringing again catches me swallowing back a yawn. If it is the casual call of some pal of course I can explain that I have been having a siesta, but if it is Frederika. . . . I had told her that I was going to be busy all day which is in a sense the truth.

With two rings to go I locate and extract a hair from my mouth, lower my legs to the ground and stand up. For a second the room slips sideways. I grasp the edge of the bunk until the telegraph wires in my head stop singing. Patently I should not have had that audit ale at lunch time. The bell peals again, hideously shattering the silence, unpardonably penetrating the only thing I thought I could call my own – privacy.

I stumble across the room smoothing back my hair and just manage to snatch the receiver as it starts to ring for the sixth time. Such is the hysteria behind my grab that the instrument nearly slips out of my hand and, in juggling with it, catching it, and getting it up to my ear the wrong side up, another three whole seconds pass. By now my heart is thumping audibly and irregularly and my breath comes loud as I open my mouth to say 'Hullo'.

That is to say I open mouth to say the word but no sound comes forth. I try a second time, louder. The muscular effort, impeded by an obstacle of phlegm, makes a strange sound which I hope will be attributed to a technical fault on the line. Up to a point my hopes are justified.

'Hullo, are you Battersea 0849?'

The voice is female and accusatory. Of necessity I clear my throat before answering, 'Yes it is.'

'Peter, is that you?'

'Yes, who's that?'

Again the accusatory tone. 'Well, who do you suppose it is?'

Another heavy throat clearance and, 'Frederika, I didn't - er, ah - how are you, darling?'

'How are *you*, Peter? I was beginning to think I had got a wrong number.'

'Did you - I mean were you?'

'Peter, are you all right?'

I hear Frederika's voice change key from flat to very sharp. 'You sound odd,' she says.

'Odd? Do I?'

'Yes, you *do*. What are you doing?'

'Doing? Nothing, darling. Why?'

'I thought you said you wanted to be alone because you were going to write.'

'I have - I mean I am. That is, I am writing now.'

'Then why do you say you are doing nothing?'

'Darling, I meant that I wasn't doing anything *except* writing.'

There is a short but penetrating pause. 'Why did you sound so peculiar just now?'

I make a deprecatory nasal noise intended to dismiss as an absurdity that I sounded peculiar.

'Have you got a cold, Peter?'

'No. I don't think I've got a cold, darling.'

'You were so long coming to the 'phone, I thought perhaps you were not feeling well and were lying down.'

17

'Good Lord no. I was – I just. . . .'

Shackled now by my ear I look round for a chair and see one just out of reach, but the increasingly censorious tone in Frederika's voice calls me smartly back to attention.

'Peter, are you there?'

'Yes, darling, here I am.'

'Your voice sounds so strange this afternoon. Are you sure that nothing is wrong?'

'Of course, why should there be?'

'Just that you sound so different, that's all.'

'Different? Different from what exactly?'

Sleep has now receded and a petulant edge, aggravated by my inability to sit, creeps into my voice.

'What do you mean, I sound different, Frederika?'

'Well . . . you just sound – odd, that's all.'

I dare a pawn's offensive – one pace forward. 'Well that's hardly very specific, is it?'

A brief pause follows this counter-attack, a pause long enough for the glove of challenge to be picked off the floor. I profit by the moment to reach for the chair. Twisting round, I nearly pull a muscle in my back and only just regain my balance without dropping the receiver.

Outside the studio the twilight blackbird lands on a fragile branch and stays there maintaining its balance by extravagant oscillations of its tail. From this standpoint it embarks upon a protracted and aggressive trill indicating to local cats that it has done with the business of the day.

My attention is recalled by a new and dangerously objective note in Frederika's voice.

'Peter, darling. Tell me something.'

'Yes?'

'Have you got anyone with you?'

'What do you mean with me? You mean with me here?'

'Yes' – voice small, sweet and innocent – 'Have you?'

This is a recognizable and all too familiar stage in our telephone procedure when I know there is no longer anything to be gained by playing safe. It is the moment when the man suffering from vertigo throws himself over the edge rather than suffer the un-

18

certainty of clinging on; when the soldier in battle rushes on towards the enemy and certain death rather than suffer continuous bombardment in the relative safety of a trench; when the small boy with puny fists attacks the big bully knowing he must in any case be beaten up. Now more with relief than anger I let myself go.

'God almighty, how do you think I spend my afternoons? Pleasuring chorus-girls? Deflowering virgins? Can't you accept the fact that I have work to do?'

'You weren't working when I rang you just now, were you?'

'For God's sake, Frederika. I have been working the whole bloody day except for a beer and a sandwich at lunch time. What palsied thing are you trying to suggest?'

'Please try not to lose your temper, Peter. It doesn't suit you.'

'God damn it, woman, I am not losing my temper. I only want to know what we are arguing about, that's all.'

'*I'm* not arguing, darling. I only want you to be honest with me and tell me who the woman is you've got with you.'

I draw a deep breath through white, dilated nostrils. I need the oxygen. 'Oh, is that all you want to know? Well, since you ask, there are a couple of red-hot Creole women waiting for me upstairs in bed.'

'Trying to be funny doesn't suit you, Peter.'

'Hell and damnation! According to you nothing I ever do suits me.'

'If you raise your voice I can't hear what you are saying – which is probably just as well because when you cool down a bit you'll probably regret the cruel things you have just said.'

By now my ear is suctioned to the instrument like a plunger to a blocked drain. I turn, making an involuntary gesture of despair to the empty room. It is now quite dark.

As if to emphasize the fall of night the blackbird throws up its tail and precipitates itself into flight with a loud and startling shrill. By contrast Frederika's next speech sounds distant and unreal.

'If you choose to lead a sordid life, Peter, that is no concern of mine. But what I cannot bear is you lying to me.'

Now it is my turn to play piano.

'For pity's sake, Frederika, hold on to your reason – even if I'm losing mine. . . . Listen to me for a moment. As a result of this endless and ridiculous conversation I am now in total darkness and if you don't mind I want to go and turn on a light.'

'Can't you talk in the dark?'

'No I cannot.'

'Of course one has to remember that you have rather poor powers of concentration.'

'I was doing all right before you rang.'

'Yes, I am *sure* you were.'

'What do you mean by that?'

'Well you must have been concentrating very hard to have taken so long to answer the telephone.'

'What the hell are you trying to infer? You've just said I've no powers of concentration. Now you're contradicting yourself.'

'That's not true.'

'What in the name of God does truth mean talking to a woman like you? I am going to turn on the light.'

I hear myself starting to shout and so try to get some enjoyment out of it.

'I feel the need for LIGHT.'

I bang the receiver down on the desk and lunge for the light-switch. In the dark my extended middle finger hits the switch-block hard, bending back the nail and tearing it from the quick. The light turned on reveals the forming of a purple blood-clot. Cursing, and sucking the finger, I return to the desk and pick up the receiver. I hear the loaded silence at the other end. The pain in my finger makes me speak in a low and emotional voice.

'Are you still there, darling?' I say.

Once again Frederika mistakes the signals relayed through the wire.

'Yes,' she answers in a voice that indicates that she might – just might – be prepared to accept an apology: that is if it is lengthy and grovelling enough. 'Yes,' she says, 'I am still here.'

I think my next sentence is as much a surprise to me as to her.

'Well then,' I hear myself saying, 'why don't you go to hell?'

2

How to describe it? Is it memory, or just memory of a memory? It is like a ticker-tape this memory, starting, stopping, pausing and going on again. Sometimes there are long deliveries. Often they are scrambled or mutilated. But how to describe it?

At first it is my rocking-horse. I am astride it galloping, galloping. It is a lovely feeling, but now it has become my boat, the boat I sail in the Municipal Gardens. I am astride it sailing faster and faster. It is the most sublime feeling. Faster and faster we go, then suddenly the lovely feeling stops and there is only a throbbing between my legs like hiccups. This throbbing goes on for quite a long time. When I wake up it is morning. There is sun on the white wall, and blue sky, and a pale green apple. It is blissful but it doesn't last because I have got to go for a walk to the Rocks with the new nanny. She always wants to go for a walk to the Rocks but I don't like this because she leaves me strapped in my push-chair in the sun while she talks to the Corporal on a bench under a tree. They always talk about the same thing.

'When is it going to be, Joe?' says my nanny. 'When can we put up the banns?'

'I don't know, dear,' he says. 'I'll have to ask the C.O.'

So it is the Rocks every day with the same old question and answer, while I sit in the sun in my push-chair getting hot. Sometimes I wet my nappy which is first hot then cool, or so my memory tells me. Was I, I wonder, overlong in nappies?

There are times when I have to go out with my mother. Then I have to wear the tussore suit and tussore hat and white buckskin shoes to match. The nanny often buckles in a bit of skin when she uses the button-hook to strap up the shoes but I am more concerned with the fact that no other boy of two wears white buckskin shoes and a matching tussore suit anyway. My mother takes me to the Garden of Gethsemane. There is a nice old monk there with a long beard and a rope round his waist who smiles out of the top of his beard. He takes me for a walk under the old olive trees there and doesn't seem to notice the tussore suit or shoes.

At other times I go for a ride on my donkey, Dounia. This is led by Dina whom my father calls Vladimir, usually in an impatient voice. Dina is a jolly refugee with a black moustache who likes to play tricks on the nanny. Sometimes he comes into the bedroom in the mornings while she is still in bed. Then he tries to pinch her breasts which are usually showing. Nanny pretends to make a fuss and he goes out laughing. He never shuts the door by using the handle but always pulls it by the latch. One day I was walking back to the house with my nanny and I tripped and fell on my face in some sick. As if that wasn't enough nanny smacked me hard. Even now I have an abnormal revulsion from vomit and excreta.

We live in the Muristan, in the Old City, and often Arabs squat to do their business on top of the wall beside our house. They don't use paper and they don't seem to mind anybody seeing them either. My nanny usually makes a fuss about this and tells my mother that she wants to give notice. Whenever she goes to give notice my mother gets very cross and nanny ends up crying. I seem to cry most when I have my hair cut because the barber always pulls small bits of hair. The other time I cry is during Ramadan when they let off guns every night which frighten me. Once when we were out walking we passed an Indian soldier with a rifle standing outside a gate. I asked my nanny what he did. She told me that he made the bangs at Ramadan, so I was frightened and made a fuss every time I had to go that way again.

I am frightened of the dark and I cry in bed at night. If I don't stop crying, my nanny says, the Bogy Man will come in at the window. Then she turns the light out. Sometimes my mother comes in and asks me what I am crying about. I tell her that I can see pictures in the dark, but she doesn't seem to understand what I mean. Once I told my father about these pictures in the dark but he didn't understand either. How can a child explain 'imagination' before he knows what the word means?

We have a black servant in the house. He is quite black with three even blacker slits in each cheek. My father calls him the *safragi* or sometimes the Berbereen, but his name is Ahmed. Ahmed wears a red tarbush and a very long white *galabeyah*. I asked Ahmed if his bottom was black too. He didn't answer but simply bent over and lifted up his galabeyah. It was as black as chocolate. There is a house-boy too but he is white. He is always down in the cistern, pumping water. I watch him do this often but he seldom speaks. Once, after he had left, I heard my father telling my mother that he wasn't a boy at all, but a girl. She was a refugee from Russia and her whole family had been killed under her nose but somehow she had managed to escape. Everybody who isn't English seems to be a refugee except Miss Larson from the American Colony – and of course the Arabs and the Jews.

My mother has got a new dog, a white saluki given to her by an emir. The saluki is called Rhoda and she comes into my nursery sometimes. One day I peed on the floor and said it was Rhoda. I felt very unhappy about this for a long time afterwards because Rhoda was taken out and smacked. I ate some cigarettes one day and got smacked too. I think I did it because I couldn't make the smoke come out of the other end and eating them was the only way to make them get smaller. Here the memory-scrambler is at work because I keep getting messages about a hippopotamus at the Cairo Zoo called Mr Cream. Or was it called Peter? Anyway, it was some joke of my father's and quite irrelevant.

My mother and father go out a lot at night and I am put to bed in two armchairs placed face to face. A nice Armenian woman comes in specially to do this and I always feel quite happy when she is there. My mother is very tall and has long beads which come down to her stomach. She always smells of powder which comes out of a box with pictures of powder-puffs on the outside. My father has a gramophone with a picture of a small white dog on it. He often plays a tune about a blue bird and sings at the same time to the gramophone which spoils the music. Sometimes he dances a bit too. On occasion he wears riding breeches but they don't look very good on him like they do on Peake Pasha. Peake Pasha is a friend of my mother's and we go for visits to his house in Transjordan. I enjoy this because he makes my mother let me have two eggs for breakfast and I am not forced to eat spinach or marrow for lunch. Marrow actually makes me sick and I can't get the dog to eat it either. The sun is always shining when we go to stay with Peake Pasha and the sky is always blue. When we go riding in the desert my mother and Peake go in front and I ride behind with the Arab galloper who holds me and the reins in one hand, and a lance with a pennon in the other. The saddle is hard and the Arab holds me very tight but I don't mind this at all because it is such a fine feeling to be out in the desert on a horse with the wind blowing and the sun up in the blue sky. In the house is a golden apricot, or is it a peach?

The scrambler again: suddenly we are at a place called El Kantara by the Nile, is it? Or by a railway station? It is sunset and there are dhows with lateen sails and camels. Perhaps it is the Canal. I remember also spinach for lunch.

Now it is my third birthday and I have been taken into my mother's and father's bedroom to be given some presents. The nicest is made out of wood and string by some Russian refugees. It is a board with wooden chickens that peck when you swing the ball that is attached underneath by string. My father is sitting on top of the bed picking his toes. He is complaining to my mother about the Muezzin just opposite our house and says he gets woken up every morning at the same time by the Imam saying his prayers. My mother asks him why he doesn't put wax in his ears. My father says he does but the prayers still wake him. Personally I like the sound of the Muezzin which is very soothing and musical. (Recently I heard it again in Rabat. I was woken at four in the morning by the noise borne in on the light air, haunting, melodious and strange; the most musical sound I have ever heard.)

Soon I am to go in a P & O called the *Sphinx*. I do not at this time know what a P & O is but I know it means that I have got to have an inoculation. I don't like the sound of the inoculation because my mother says it won't hurt. I am sure it will because my mother says the barber won't hurt either. I believe I am to go on the P & O by myself.

Tonight the jackals are barking. This is another good sound.

*　　*　　*

Himmbaersaft, Alpenrosen, Eierspeise, Gnädigefrau, Schpitzbuben, Gugelhupf, Todtesgebirge . . . these are just code-words that I feed into the computer to provoke appetites and desires; memories in time and place.

The rain is sheeting down in straight lines. It is coming down so hard that it throws up little fountains of mud where it hits the earth. The grey lake is pocked with huge rain drops so that it looks more like a sheet of lead than a sheet of water. A single *plätte* is the only boat I can see. The man standing up in the stern is pushing the up-curved bow over the lead with a huge stern oar. I can't hear the boat over the noise of the rain, but I can see the man pushing and pushing, and I can see the rise and fall of the big blade cutting in an out of the sheet of lead.

I am sitting under the gable end of the villa watching Otto splitting logs. Like all the houses in the Salzkammcrgut one eave of the roof is extended to make a wood store and this is where I am sitting watching Otto at work. Otto is a big boy, nearly fourteen, and can almost do a man's work, but he says he is going to be a schoolmaster in Linz when he is older; not just a peasant like his father. He is very pleased with the way he splits logs, though, and laughs every time he does it exactly with one blow. Otto wears clogs, the sort with wooden bottoms and leather tops. When he goes into the house he leaves his clogs neatly under the eaves and walks in his stockinged feet. I would like some clogs but my grandmother says only peasants wear them. A rain drop comes through the roof above where I am sitting and makes a dark mark on my *lederhosen*. Actually they are not *lederhosen* because they are not made of *leder*. They are imitation *lederhosen*. Now, Otto who is a peasant has real *lederhosen* but I have only imitation ones. If a drop of rain fell on Otto's *lederhosen* it wouldn't show because they are made of real *leder* and, in any case, they are very shiny because he wipes his hands on them after meals. I asked why I couldn't have real *lederhosen* and my grandmother said it was because we were very badly off. Are we poorer than the peasants then? I would be quite content if I had real *lederhosen* and a pair of clogs which I could take off when I come into the house. The *gammsbardt* (that's the shaving-brush thing) in my green hat isn't a real one either.

My grandmother is very greedy. She has a trembling lip and a trembling hand but she always manages to get the rings of butter safely on to her plate at breakfast. There is never quite enough butter, however. My grandmother says we can't afford it, but she trots down to Fischer's every day between breakfast and lunch-time to eat the fresh cakes. Sometimes, if she thinks she is going to miss the best fresh pastries, she actually breaks into a run, carrying her umbrella at the trail like a rifle. I am told it is bad to eat between meals.

The food we have is certainly very good and sometimes we go to Frischmuth's, the hotel on the lake. In the restaurant there is a tank with fish called *saibling* swimming about in it. My grand-mother usually picks out the one she wants to eat and calls over the Herr Ober and talks to him in German. She's an Austrian herself so this is no problem for her. I too can talk Austrian, but only peasant dialect which I have learnt from Otto and the other boys. My grandmother is always correcting my German which makes her friends laugh at bridge parties. But regional accents are good and I well understand a man's love for the free and easy sounds he lets out of his mouth.

Saibling must be one of the world's best fish to eat. They are pink inside and we have them with boiled potatoes and melted butter. I could always eat more but my father says they are very expensive and I can fill up on something else. I am allowed plenty of *rindfleisch*, or boiled beef, which we have with redcurrant jam, lovely sour *schwartzbrodt* and a cucumber salad with caraway seeds. There is also a very good soup with ham dumplings in it. For special treats we have *sachertorte* which is a special chocolate cake with jam inside, but my grandmother gets most of this. My father is always very attentive to her and feeds her up with all the best of everything.

I enjoy most going for *ausflüge*, or picnics in the mountains. We can only do this when it is not raining, of course, but there is always plenty to eat because my grandmother doesn't come. The trouble is I get very thirsty, but my father says it is bad to drink too much when climbing mountains. I carry my own ruck-sack with a jersey and one or two packets of food in it and am equipped with an alpenstock with two or three metal labels nailed to it of mountains I have climbed. Unfortunately, from my point of view, we never stop early enough for lunch and the last hour's climb is agony from hunger and thirst. The best things on the picnic are always the *schinkensemmeln*. These are fresh crusty rolls stuffed with butter and soft pink ham drooping out of the edges. My father says the *semmeln* are made from the best flour in the world. My grandfather, who is a Hungarian, says this is not quite true because the best flour in the world comes from Hungary. My grandfather is much taller and better-looking than my father and always smells of stuff called Après l'Ondée, but although he is a fine man he doesn't come on the longer climbs because he says he thinks he should keep Mrs Hoyte company. Mrs Hoyte is a beautiful American lady with white skin covered in freckles. She is also very charming but she is stone deaf and has to lip-read. I don't mind sitting and letting her lip-read me because she is so extremely nice. The only time I have ever seen my grandfather get angry was when I said her red-painted fingernails looked like claws. He told me then that I must never, never pass personal remarks and I felt deeply ashamed for a long time afterwards.

Sometimes my father takes Mausi on an *ausflug* with us. Mausi is a very pretty girl with a mole on the inside of her left breast. I often wonder if there are any more lower down and I must admit that I would quite like to have a look to see. I even wonder if my father has the same idea, but I rather doubt it. Mausi always wears the *steyretracht*; that is the dirndl and the low-cut blouse well designed for showing-off the mole. Once when we were climbing down from the Trislvant, which is a mountain with a cliff-face falling straight down into the lake, my father said I could run on ahead by myself if I wanted to. The paths are all marked by coloured splashes of paint on the trees, so it is perfectly easy to find the way, but I didn't particularly feel like going on ahead so I stayed with them.

The mountains in the Salzkammergut are very lovely and make everybody feel good – that is, when you are up in them. Sometimes the cowherds and woodcutters are so happy all by themselves in the mountains that they let out a special sort of whoop which starts on a top note and goes right down the scale. Then they listen to themselves echoing back and forth across the valley. I could probably do this sort of whoop if my voice had broken, but you need a man's voice for it. People you meet in the mountains will always wish you '*grüss Gott*', which means 'God's greeting'. In spring and summer you get wild narcissus and cyclamen on the lower slopes. My father is very fond of these and goes round sniffing them all day long and presenting them to his mother and Mausi. Personally I prefer looking for the different sorts of gentian. Some are quite easy to find, but my favourite is rather rare and only grows high up. It is the most beautiful blue I have ever seen and it gives me quite a strange sensation inside if I stare at it for long. I have been up higher than 8,000 feet where you can get edelweiss but I have never found one yet. Some of the older boys know where to get them but they won't tell me because they sell them to the tourists. I have never come across a chamois either, though I passed a man once coming down from the Todtesgebirge carrying one over his shoulder. It had its throat cut wide open, a gaping red slash across its brown fur.

Sometimes we come across big patches of wild strawberries which are especially delicious for breakfast. They bring them in on a bed of leaves and serve them with fine white sugar. There is another sort of round black berry which is very refreshing if you've got the patience to collect a lot before stuffing them into your mouth. They leave your lips stained purple, but I like them best baked in a tart or rolled up in a pancake. My father likes *reinunken* for breakfast, which is a sort of smoked eel.

The pine forests smell lovely. Some people make miniature gardens in the moss with paths and streams and stepping stones and many of them have water-pianos. These are quite easy to make. All you need is a mountain stream, a small wooden water-wheel and half a dozen or so bottles. On one end of the water-wheel you put a roller with pegs which move a number of trip-hammers. Then you fill the bottles with various levels of water so that when the wheel goes round the hammers strike the bottles and play a tune. This music coming out of the woods sounds very pretty and it costs practically nothing. Sometimes you get men who come round the village with a sort of suitcase in which stemmed glasses are fixed. They fill the glasses up to different levels and play a tune by rubbing their fingers round the rims. Of course they do this for money. But the best time of all is during the *seefest*. . . . Then everybody goes out on the lake in the big *plätten* decorated with lights and sing and yodel and play the accordion. This is the time you see the prettiest girls, but one can't really get near them because they are always surrounded by big, shouting men who think nothing of giving one a good shove out of the way.

*   *   *

My brother has just been born. This is good news though I shall not be able to see him for a while. He is going to be called Michael Charles Deane. The Deanes are on my mother's side and have some connexion with Ireland.

*   *   *

I have just seen Micky. He wears a net cap to keep his ears from sticking out and the nanny won't let me touch him. We are staying in my grandfather's flat in Victoria which is extremely dark and gloomy. I wish Mrs Hoyte were here but she has gone back to America. I don't know where my grandmother is. Micky's nanny and the maid are always grumbling together in the kitchen and call my grandfather 'the foreigner'. My mother comes in sometimes to use my grandfather's telephone. When she is telephoning she often calls herself Miss Fremlin, her maiden name, which annoys my father. Also she smokes gaspers which annoys him even more because he only smokes Turks.

*   *   *

This place is called Woodcut Farm. There is a girl here called Joyce who is a year older than me and she is so beautiful that she makes me feel sick. This afternoon Micky was standing up in his cot annoying me so I gave him a whack on the bare bottom with a wooden spoon. Unfortunately the nanny caught me, smacked me hard and sent me to bed.

Now, it is a beautiful summer night and very hot. All the doors and windows are open and the air smells of roses and hay. Joyce is in the next room with the door open and I am wondering whether I dare get out of bed and go and give her a kiss. It takes me a long time to get up enough courage, but it is still not quite dark and she looks so beautiful lying there asleep with only a sheet over her. I tiptoe over and kiss her cheek. It is wet with sweat, which surprises me. I run back to my own room quickly

29

before I get caught. Joyce won't know tomorrow that I have kissed her and it wasn't really worth it anyway. Yesterday we all saw an aeroplane.

*   *   *

We have got our own flat in Victoria now. It is even darker than my grandfather's, but a nice woman called Ines has come to look after me. Her brother works in a chocolate factory and he is allowed as many chocolates as he can eat. Ines says he gets sick of them but I find this hard to believe. I share a room with Ines and when she goes to bed at night she takes off all her clothes and she looks beautiful. One of these days I am going to ask her to let me touch her breasts which are big and soft-looking. Actually I am in love with Betty Balfour who is an actress and I often see her in the cinema which Ines takes me to. I pray every night to be allowed to marry her when I grow up. My grandfather took me to see *The Battle of Mons*. There was a Highlander who put his wounded comrade in a wheelbarrow to save him from the Boche. There were a lot of men, all dog-tired after a long march, who just fell down and slept where they lay. But they were in grave danger because the Bosches were very close behind them and the officer knew this but he couldn't get the men to wake up. So he and the sergeant went off to a toy shop and bought a toy drum and a penny whistle. Then the officer and the sergeant played the regimental march on the drum and penny whistle so that all the soldiers got up and marched off just in time. There was also a gunner officer keeping the guns firing to the last man and the last round. While he was doing this he saw 'the Angel of Mons'. My grandfather said he knew that officer, but only laughed when I asked him about the Angel.

Another time Ines took me to see Ramon Novarro in *Ben Hur* at the Tivoli. This was a horrible story about galley-slaves being flogged to death, or being chained to their oars when the ship sank. I had the programme for a long time afterwards and even the smell of the shiny paper brought back terrible memories of the slaves and the Roman soldiers spilling the drinking water just out of Ben Hur's reach.

What Ines and I like best is the Victoria Palace just down the

30

road. They are mostly comedians like old Nellie Wallace, Harry Lauder, George Robey and Seymour Hicks. There is also a woman who dresses up in a man's evening clothes called Hetty King. We also saw a play there called *Where the Rainbow Ends*. The best thing in it was an old gardener who kept on saying 'I'm barmy. I'm barmy'. Next week we are going to see *Peter Pan*. The trouble now is that Ines does all her undressing underneath her nightie. I think this is because I asked her to let me touch her breasts.

*   *   *

Hack no furniture.
Xenophon is a Greek.

Somebody is whimpering in the rhododendrons. I am unhappy already but this makes me feel frightened as well. 'You're just a filthy little New Kid,' I can hear someone saying. That's P. A. Stamford's voice. He is the worst bully in the school.

'Boot him again, Hollis,' Stamford says.

I can hear the sound of Hollis booting. He plays Right Back for the Second Eleven and is a very good kick.

'That's what you get for being a New Kid, see,' says Stamford.

I am a new kid too, I keep thinking. P. A. Stamford hates all new kids – in fact I think he hates nearly everybody except those who are nearly as good at bullying as he is. He doesn't touch Dorrien-Smith, though. Dorrien-Smith is very fierce but he isn't a bully. He sometimes punches one in the wind when passing, but this is just because he is a natural fighter. He doesn't do it to be unkind. Dorrien-Smith comes from the Scilly Isles which is possibly what makes him so fierce and tough.

This school is hidden in pine trees and rhododendrons. I wonder how many tears have been shed in these rhododendrons. Buckets and buckets I should think. I swear I'll never plant rhododendrons when I grow up.

The term has only just started and I won't see my mother again for all this term, all next holidays, all next term – and not till the holidays after that. She's abroad with my father. I don't know where I shall be going for the holidays. I can't really imagine such a long time but I suppose it will end some time. I could stand it better if it weren't for P. A. Stamford and Hollis. Why can't they just leave one alone?

Tritton is my best friend, and after Tritton, Peacock. Tritton's elder brother is getting married next week to somebody called Judy Hurt. I've seen a photograph of her and she looks frightfully pretty. Tritton is being allowed out for the wedding. He sleeps in the next bed to me in the dorm. Warde-Aldam *ma* is captain of our dorm and flicks one with a wet towel if one's not getting on with it – and even if one is. Warde-Aldam *mi* is quite nice but he never gets flicked by his brother. After lights Tritton and I have bets on who can hold their breath the longest. Sometimes we shoot daddy-long-legs on the ceiling with our garters. I don't know how I am going to stand all these weeks and months here. It would be better without all the rhododendrons and pine trees – and without P. A. Stamford and Hollis of course.

Foxy looks fierce but he is very decent really. He always ties his tie in a big knot and wears plus-fours. He plays golf a lot and did something brave in the Great War. I asked him if he had ever seen the Angel of Mons, and he just laughed. It's the opposite with old Apps (he's the other headmaster). He looks very kind, but he isn't really – nor is his wife though she is very pi. She plays the piano for prayers every night in a long brown dress. She looks very hard at the music and has a drip on the end of her long nose. Foxy's wife is very nice and friendly but we don't see her so much because she's got children. Every morning when old Apps takes roll-call, he starts off, 'Good evening, gentlemen – and others.' I laughed about the first half a dozen times. Now I have given up because I know he counts me among the 'others'. When Apps swishes he really hurts, but Foxy only gives one a tap or two. Perhaps it is because after being in the war he doesn't want to inflict any more pain. I bet old Apps never went near the war.

Bothamwetham has got hair on his cock, but he is much bigger than most of us. You can see it when we go for cold baths. We have cold baths every morning even if it is snowing outside. There is always a monitor there to flick us with a wet towel if we don't go in properly. P. A. Stamford is an absolute expert with a wet towel. He can practically take your skin off.

Gepp's just come back from having his appendix out. He says it hurt frightfully. I am absolutely dreading getting appendicitis. Gepp says you can always tell if you have got it because you want to go to the lavatory terribly and when you get there all you can do is fart. He has got a red scar on the right side of his stomach which looks like a caterpillar.

James's sister has just got married. He says that his sister told him that when you get married a man's cock gets stiff and he is allowed to poke it into the woman's thing. I absolutely don't believe it. Imagine old Apps sticking his cock into Mrs Apps! Well, one can't really imagine it, can one? Actually I wouldn't mind sticking mine into Elsie, the maid. She's got big bubs and is very nice. Sometimes she gives me an extra sausage on Sundays. The trouble is my cock never goes stiff, but that probably only happens after getting married, if one can believe James. If it was anybody else but James, I would think they were having me on.

We have got an epidemic and Gurney *mi* has just died. Peacock and I feel very sorry for his parents, but they have still got Gurney *ma* left and I believe there is a *minimus* still at home. Everybody is getting mastoid and it hurts most frightfully. I am dreading getting mastoid. I would almost rather have appendicitis, but I dread that too – plus Hollis and P. A. Stamford of course. Also I may be going to get the swish from Budgie who swishes harder than anybody. So now I have got four things to dread – no five. I had forgotten about telling the time. The thing is that I haven't got a very mathematical brain and I can't tell the time too easily. The trouble is that my desk is nearest the door and sometimes Foxy sends me out to tell him the time by the school clock so that he can put his watch right. I dread doing this because then I have to hang about in the hall till Elsie or someone comes along. Then I have to pretend that I am not sure that the school clock is right, so that she, or whoever it is, has to check it with their own watch. By the time I get back into the classroom Foxy wants to know what the dickens I have been doing all this time.

Montague-Douglas-Scott is very good at drawing, but whenever I say anything funny he passes it on and pretends he made it up himself. Anderson has got very thick glasses and terribly muscular calves, just like a man's. His looks make me feel sick.

Poor Walker never speaks to anybody. He just spends his time chasing butterflies with a cricket bat. I suppose you could say he is 'bats'. Neville *ma* is quite nice but he just grits his teeth and drives the ball at you as hard as he can. That's another thing to dread, fielding practice when Neville takes it. There is a new master called Mr Curtis who takes us for maths. He tries to be nice to me and puts his arm round my shoulder when he is correcting my work. This is very embarrassing, particularly as his breath stinks of pipe tobacco.

Next Sunday is 'Blub Sunday'. 'Blub Sunday' is the day when everybody pays off old scores. At least that's the idea, but actually it is just an excuse for the bullies to get at anybody. I am told that I am certain to be made to blub on Sunday. Peacock and I have made a pact to stick very close together and come to the defence of the other one if he is attacked first. I hope I have the guts to stick up for Peacock if he is attacked and not me. When 'Blub Sunday' comes, I'm just going to pretend it is not 'Blub Sunday' but a Sunday like any other Sunday. I wonder who had the brainy wheeze to invent 'Blub Sunday'. P. A. Stamford, I suppose.

*   *   *

Schofield has run away! Apparently Schofield's mother has been to see Foxy and told him why. Apparently it was because he was being bullied by Hollis and P. A. Stamford and he just couldn't stand it any more. It wouldn't be much good me running away because my parents are abroad.

The whole school is buzzing with excitement. Foxy is going to talk to the whole school at eleven o'clock. I wonder what it is all about.

*   *   *

This is the best day of my whole life! P. A. Stamford has been demonitorized! Foxy said it had come to his ears that there had been some bad cases of bullying lately and that he wasn't going to have it in his school. He said that it had also come to his ears that the principal offender was P. A. Stamford and that, in order to make a public example of him, he was to be demonitorized. Stamford was sitting there just next to Foxy. He looked just the

34

same as usual, only a little paler. This is a tremendous weight off my mind. What about Hollis though?

Every night I am hungry. After I have said my prayers I lie awake for hours thinking of the sausages we have on Sundays. I wonder when this misery will all end. One can only bear it because there's nothing – absolutely nothing – else one can do.

3

Allegro con spirito (*Tempo di Barcarola*)

> *Thanks to the bounteous sitter*
> *Who sat not at all on his seat.*
> *Down with the beer that's bitter,*
> *Up with the wine that's sweet.*
> *And oh! that some generous critter*
> *Would give us more ducks to eat!*

> *Carving with elbow nudges,*
> *Lobsters we throw behind.*
> *Vinegar nobody grudges,*
> *Lower boys drink it blind;*
> *Sober as so many judges,*
> *We'll give you a bit of our mind.*

Which being the certified true copy, believe it or not, of verses 3 and 4 of the *Eton Boating Song*. AUTHOR ANON.

Classical Report for Lent School-time 1933

NAME: Luke   8th out of 23

He has been away so much that this result is partly guess-work. And I cannot help feeling that he has been lucky to be placed so high. For his Latin is not sound, and in school he has shown himself very slow at picking up any new ideas. But although he seems stupid, his ability for writing English is above the average. His Sunday Questions have been excellent and History has been well done. He takes great trouble to learn the facts and he can express his ideas on paper. So for his English work and for his industry he deserves this place. His good temper and friendliness makes him a pleasant boy to teach.

F. W. How

Eheu! fugaces, Postume, Postume

Dear Mayes,

Luke has my sympathy, for he must spend more hours *at* work than any boy in the school. I purposely do not say 'working', because I do not think that he can really be working all the time. I find it hard to believe that he can be so slow, and I am pretty sure that his mind wanders a good deal. I must admit that the quality of his work is not wholly bad – he has to have a good deal of help to shorten the hours of Pupil Room. I am not certain how much of the new things he learns remains with him, for he is in every way incredibly forgetful. I do not know how to cure him of the awful habit he has of bringing in wrong books, losing everything, showing up work at the wrong time. He has not sufficient time to do a punishment! and so I curse gloomily at him. Provided things go smoothly, he keeps up fairly well, but when he has anything to rattle him, he is rattled with a vengeance. I believe he learns more than he appears to do and that the rate of progress is not wholly unsatisfactory. He is willing enough and incredibly patient and cheerful, nor does he resent (apparently) having to spend so much of his time in Pupil Room. I shorten it to the best of my power – but it is a hard task to drag him through the minimum of work.

Yours sincerely,
W. G. Tatham

Labuntur anni: nec Pietas moram

Classical Report for Summer School-time 1933

NAME: Luke   Place: 15th out of 27

He has been a good deal absent and I have no doubt that his place would have been higher had this not been so. As it is, his work has been very definitely an affair of darkness contrasted with light. His Latin seems to me rather strikingly weak, especially in prose where he has rarely scored over thirty per cent in marks. On the other hand his History and Divinity have been generally good and his English always so. His Essays show a natural sense of style, and both in manner and matter are easily among the best in the division. His mind works slowly and I think that, in Latin especially, he has often found the pace to be more than he can manage. I hope that he will manage to improve both his pace and his memory. Meanwhile, I think that he has worked quite hard in this division and deserves credit for such good work as he has done.

E. J. Cruso

Rugis et instanti Senectae
Afferet, indomitaeque Morti.

ETON COLLEGE, WINDSOR, December 15, 1933

Dear Mayes,
Many of my pupils are incompetent at managing their own affairs but Luke is far the most incompetent – and the most irritating in this way. Always late, always without the right books, always behindhand with his work, he is a trial to me in Pupil Room, as he is to his division masters. In desperation, I have to give him a great deal of help. His slowness is due to the fact that he has no idea of concentration and hard work. He has the ability to appear awake and actually to be asleep. I find sometimes that in half an hour he has written down ten words for verses and done nothing else. Though he is extremely weak in other subjects, he is not desperately bad at Latin. He is fairly accurate as a rule and only rarely makes stupid mistakes. He is quite willing and cheerful in spite of misfortunes. In his own mind he must know that he really has himself to blame as much as anybody.

I am afraid he has not had a very good half.

Yours sincerely,
W. G. Tatham

Non, si trecenis quotquot eunt dies,
Amice, places illacrimabilem

ETON COLLEGE, WINDSOR, December, 1935

(To Sir Harry Luke)

Dear Luke,
. . . Of his position in the house I am less certain, for he is the dominant character in his group of friends, and the group is not

doing well. Apart from removing his battery of pipes and tobacco I have had nothing against him, but from three different sources has come the suggestion – entirely vague – that his influence was not especially good, and I mention it without endorsing it.* It will probably be a good thing to move his room next half and so modify his environment slightly.

Yours sincerely,
Charles Mayes

*I should point out that there is no question of morals involved.

> *Plutona tauris; qui ter amplum*
> *Geryonen Tityonque tristi*

ETON COLLEGE, WINDSOR, March 29, 1935

Dear Mayes,

Last half the task of writing Luke's report was a pleasant one. He seemed to have turned over a new leaf and to be making progress. This half it is far from pleasant. However much I rack my brains, I can find nothing to praise. He has constantly been in trouble and was very lucky to escape a complaint. Instead of making an effort to do better, he has made endless excuses for his bad work and tried to prove that it was not really bad. It looks very much as if he will fail in Trials, and it will be due to his shortsightedness and folly.

I have not much to complain about his work in Pupil Room; but I cannot say that his Latin has improved. I must admit also that I have found him rather irritating.

There is no need for me to continue in this strain. It is extremely disappointing.

Yours sincerely,
W. G. Tatham

> *Compescit unda, scilicet omnibus,*
> *Quicunque terrae munere vescimur,*

Mathematical Report for Summer School-time 1936

If he is to stand any chance of passing in the school certificate next half he will have to work harder, and he will also need coaching in the holidays. He is dreadfully backward and has a lazy mind.

T. H. Smyth

Enaviganda, sive reges
Sive inopes erimus coloni

Classical Report for Lent School-time 1936

Number in division: 29   Final Place: 29th out of 29

A late return, and frequent intervals of absence since are some excuses for a difficult half. But they do not anywhere near explain Luke's utterly lethargic attitude to his work. He never made the slightest attempt to catch up what he missed by his late return: he took no interest whatever in anything that we have done since: and his work has all along been on a minimum basis. The standard here has been extraordinarily low, and it is absurd to suggest that Luke is the stupidest boy in the division. I am afraid I haven't seen any sign of the very slightest effort all through the half, and I am at a loss to find a single redeeming feature.

G. Snow

Frustra cruento Marte carebimus,
Fractisque ranci fluctibus Adriae

History Report for Michaelmas School-time 1936

The most naturally idle boy I have ever met. Probably he thinks he is working, but he has no inkling of what the word work means. I cannot prophesy anything but failure for a boy so wholly ignorant of History, and one who seems to be content to remain ignorant. Nor can I pretend that, in spite of his unfailing good humour and friendliness, I have much opinion of his sense of humour. Certainly History is the last subject in which he ought to specialize.

C. R. N. Routh

Frustra per auctumnos nocentem
Corporibus metuemus Austrum

Classical Report for Lent School-time 1937

Whether the atmosphere of total incompetence with which Luke instantly involves himself on being confronted with printed matter is real or assumed is a question which this report is not going to resolve. It must suffice to say that in his hands of ever rapidly woven into an intellectual cocoon by that web of humorous dither of which he appears to possess endless resources [*sic*]. Indeed I am not sure that he has not scored a final triumph in causing me to mix the above metaphor. I fear, then, that I cannot report except unfavourably on any of his work, except perhaps music: for the echoes of his favourite instrument[1] have not infrequently beguiled us during construe schools.

J. D. Upcott

Visendus ater flumine languido
Cocytos errans, et Danai genus

Classical report for Summer School-time 1937

Idle and means to be. Sits a lumpish figure in school.

George Lyttelton

Infame, damnatusque longi
SISYPHUS *Aeolides laboris*

*   *   *

All together now, fellows; a-one, a-two, a-three:

Time ever flowing helps us be going,
Old Momma Eton, far from thee.
Hearts growing bolder, love always colder,
All but forgotten shalt thou be.

Three bronchial cheers for the Old Whore! Give her a big chilblained hand!

---

[1] Trumpet.

4

Of the King's Scholars who left Eton in the late 1930s a relatively large number showed tendencies towards homosexuality, alcoholism or suicide. Peter Luke clearly was no scholar and he left school with nothing worse after five winters in the Thames Valley than chronic bronchitis. He retained little else from that period of his life other than a mild fancy, strangely enough, for Latin verse, and an undeveloped interest in the graphic arts, which last was little to do with Eton, though the influence of a young art master, Mr Robin Darwin,[1] may have been partly responsible. Perhaps the event at Eton that had the most lasting effect on his life was the glimpse he got one day of a girl called Phoebe, the sister of a friend. What follows is Luke's own description of the first sighting of his first love.

*   *   *

From my place on the 'knife-board' I can see the visitors in the stalls – and the Beaks of course; not that anybody wants to look at them. This is the same 'knife-board' where John St Aubyn sat on the memorable occasion when in the act of buying illicit choc-ices he heard the bell ring for chapel. He had time to stuff four of them into his tail-pocket and get to his place before the 'Ram' started up the aisle. It was a hot summer's day and of course these four choc-bars melted in no time and, when he turned to pray (on the 'knife-board' you turn round to kneel inwards with your backside sticking into the gangway) a revolting brown trickle of chocolate oozed into the aisle. Of course he got flogged. It was bad luck really because one of the choc-bars was for me and another was for Andy.

But as I was saying, from my place on the 'knife-board', when I turn round to pray (ha-ha!) I can see the visitors behind me in the stalls. The stalls are of carved oak and are very beautiful. But what I saw in the stalls today nearly made me faint with beauty.

[1] Sir Robin Darwin, ARA; Rector and Vice-Provost, Royal College of Art.

It was nothing less than Andy's elder sister and he has never ever let on that he had one. She is the most beautiful creature I have ever seen – even more so than that bald Beak's wife. (It is the Beak that is bald.) I try to give her some penetrating looks but I suppose to her we are just a sea of pink boyish faces in white ties and black tail-coats.

It is quite impossible to pray here of course. In the first place Bobby Heywood-Lonsdale sits next to me and files his nails all the time – literally *all* the time – which sets my teeth perpetually on edge. Secondly Hughie Rocksavage, who sits on the other side, is constantly drawing soldiers in all sorts of different uniforms. He swaps these with Dicky Warre who is just in front of him. Warre has aptitude for illustrating revolvers, machine-guns and motor-cars. Of course when we sing that ridiculous hymn, 'Rock of Ages cleft for me' everybody yells the words 'rock-of-ages' to make them sound like Rocksavage.

There's Andy's sister again. God, isn't she beautiful! I think – and I'm not alone in this – that we should be allowed women occasionally, at least Upper Boys. (I'm now an Upper Boy.) If we were only allowed to have a woman two or three times a Half it would put a stop to seventy-five per cent of the buggery, masturbation and all that sort of business which is really rife nowadays. For example it would put Elkington, our House tart, completely out of business. After all, when you come to think of it, from the age of about fifteen onwards one is probably about as randy as one ever will be in one's whole life. At least most of my friends are. Look at Bury, he's at least nineteen and he's got a moustache. What he needs is a wife, not a moustache. Of course, traditionally the Captain of the School is allowed a wife. They say there is even a special room for her in College. But I have yet to see a Captain of the School who had the guts to claim that prerogative: 'WHAT-WE-WANT-IS-WOMEN'.

*   *   *

Andy, whose father had been killed in 1918 just before the armistice, and Peter had arrived at Eton together, they boarded together at the same House, and together they left at the end of the same Half with the absolute minimum of scholastic achievement between them. Since

Peter's parents were as usual abroad, Andy's mother kindly invited him to stay for as long as he liked, or until such time as his unpromising future was decided upon. He therefore went to stay in their flint and brick house in the Wylye Valley with the lively anticipation of getting to know the glamorous Phoebe. On arrival at Upton Lovell, wearing his newly minted Old Etonian tie, he was disappointed to discover that Phoebe was also abroad. However, there were consolations and he and Andy greatly enjoyed their new found freedom and the ancillary pleasures of smoking pipes in public, ordering pints on licensed premises and recklessly driving the ancient family Delage around the narrow lanes. Then one day. . . .

*   *   *

Phoebe is here. She has just come back from Austria, and wears a black Salzburg hat with a green cord around it which suits her terribly well. She is frightfully attractive, just as I remembered her from those days on the 'knife-board'. She thinks Andy quite ridiculous and is not a bit impressed by his success at school. All those sacrosanct titles like 'Pop' and 'Keeper of the Oppidan Wall' (if you please), she just laughs at and calls 'hearty'. Of course she lumps me with Andy. To her I am only another ex-schoolboy like him. Little does she know of the fierce fires smouldering deep within.

Phoebe is full of Austria. I try to talk to her about it but she is so full of her own experiences that she doesn't listen. Apparently she went about a lot with a fellow called Fritz. He is a count, of course, but I don't think Phoebe realizes that all Austrians who aren't peasants are counts. It seems that this Fritz is six feet five inches (I'm only a bare six feet) and used to pick her up in his arms and call her his 'Golden Child'. All I can say is that the bloody man must be extremely strong and in very good training to be able to call her his 'Golden Child' while humping her around. Phoebe is very beautiful but anyone can see that she is no featherweight. Anyway, it's no concern of mine because she is quite obviously 'beyond my degree' as the saying goes.

So we hear a good deal about Austria plus *der liebe* Fritz, and when we are not hearing about that, it's Oxford. Phoebe is an art student up at Oxford and all her friends are intellectuals. They are people like Tom Marriner, Christopher Kininmonth, Nicholas Palunin etc, and she is always going on about Auden and Isherwood. Who the hell are Auden and Isherwood, any-way? And she never stops telling you what Barnett Freedman said to her in the Ashmolean, and who she ran into in the Bodleian and who she saw bicycling down the Broad. You can imagine how this makes me feel – particularly with the news that has just come through that I have failed for the Army. Perhaps it is just as well because the mere mention of the Army makes Phoebe sneer. Besides, I think I want to be a painter.

The fact is I must now admit that I cannot look at Phoebe any more without thinking how much I would like to kiss her. I suppose that filthy Fritz has been kissing her in Austria. I wonder if he did anything else. I don't think I really want to know.

Andy teases Phoebe all the time and isn't in the least deterred by being called a 'hearty'. He just goes on teasing her merci-lessly and she gets furious, or pretends to, and attacks him physically which makes him laugh all the more. But they are very fond of each other really. I wish she wouldn't mentally lump me with him, though.

Andy's mother, Tempé, is terribly nice but she is so busy that we scarcely see her except at meals. The dogs take up a lot of her time. She has a floating population of about five or six whippets which are so in-bred that they are always having fits. They go, 'yike-yike-yike-yike-yike-yike', tearing around in ever diminishing circles until they fall down in a spasm frothing at the mouth. It is practically a daily occurrence. Then she has her stamps to do, and she also spends a lot of time with a butterfly net catching queen wasps. The idea is if you catch all the queen wasps in May they can't breed for September. Then the evenings are entirely taken up with her 'system'. She has a system on the horses which takes her hours to work out with the help of all sorts of ready-reckoners and reference books such as *Raceform* and *Ruff's Guide*, not to mention a great many newspapers. This system is only on the Flat of course. She won't touch the Sticks. Tempé says that by sticking to her system and never having a gamble she makes a profit every year. My God, she ought to, considering the time and energy she spends on it.

*　　*　　*

This sequence could be headed 'How I lost my Virginity', and though it really hasn't much to do with Phoebe's family, there is, perhaps, an indirect connexion. I was about fifteen at the time and on my way to Malta for the summer holidays with some of the Downside crowd who are well known to be rather a fast lot. The ship stopped at Marseilles and we had the day ashore. Well, when we got to the Cannebière a little chap came up to us and asked would we like to go to a *Cinema Bleu*. Of course we didn't know what a *Cinema Bleu* was but we thought we might just as well have a look, so we plodded off behind him through a lot of back-streets till we came to an unremarkable-looking door. The little bloke knocked on the door which was immediately opened by a nice-looking woman of about thirty or so who, after a lengthy conversation with this chap in French, beckoned us in. There then followed another long discussion about how much we should pay him. We didn't know what we were getting, so obviously we didn't know how much it was worth. Eventually one of the Downside boys who was a Rugby Forward said take it or leave it and your man went off looking crestfallen and hurt.

Anyway, the nice lady now took us upstairs to a hideously furnished sort of lounge where she asked us if we would like some champagne. We said no but she brought it all the same and with the champagne came, believe it or not, six or seven heavily made-up tarts (because that's what they were) in nothing but dressing-gowns. They then proceeded to parade round and round the lounge so that we could take our pick. Personally I wanted the nice lady who had showed us in, but she wasn't on the menu, apparently. Finally some ridiculous blonde chose *me*. When it had all been settled about who was to go with whom, we were ushered into another room where the blonde tried to sit on my lap while the nice lady, after several false starts, managed to get a cinema projector going.

Now this was the really hilarious bit. First we see a curly-

46

headed blonde woman (looking rather like Mary Pickford, incidentally) trotting across the Sahara Desert with a butterfly-net. This lady lepidopterist's progress is somewhat impeded by the fact that she is wearing badly cut riding breeches and a solar topee. We then cut to a Bedouin Sheik's tent where the resident Sheik, a pale young man with a black waxed moustache, is smoking a hookah. Suddenly he tenses up and looks alertly at the far horizon which is a sea of burning sand. *Ma fois!* ... what's this coming through the shimmering mirage? Well, any fool could have told him. It is the lady lepidopterist, of course, still after that poor fagged-out butterfly. Now it is but the work of a moment for the Sheik to mount his fiery steed (which looks suspiciously like the cab-horse we took from the docks to the Cannebière) and gallop across the burning *midan* in pursuit of his innocent and unsuspecting prey. 'Alas! Alack! Oh, sir, I am undone!' (Do yourself up again, madam. We are not quite ready for that yet.) The ignoble Sheik is now close upon her, gnashing his probably false teeth and rolling his eyeballs until his burnous, flying in the desert wind, blows right across his face and nearly makes him fall off his horse. But now all is lost. The butterfly is free but its erstwhile pursuer is made prisoner. (Close-up of butterfly net lying empty on burning desert sand.) It is but the work of another moment (in the cutting room) to get the lovely lepidopterist, all rolling eyes and waving riding breeches, across the saddle-bow of the stallion and gallop her back to the tent of the toothy Touareg.

By this time the Downside fellows and I were in fits and almost falling off the plush chairs. The girls were furiously trying to shush us and tell us what a beautiful film it was. But then things began to get a bit better. The Sheik starts to chase the little lady round and round his tent. She has now lost her solar topee and her blonde bubbly curls are all awry. She protests violently (this of course is a silent film) but her fate is a foregone conclusion – as we now begin to realize. By another bit of sharp work in the cutting room the Sheik very quickly manages to get her riding breeches off which, as anybody who has worn them will know, is no easy matter.

Well, here the laughter starts to die down because the Sheik, not to put too fine a point on it, starts to rummage the lady very thoroughly indeed. And she has suddenly become his not unwilling partner. So successful is this part of the film that I find myself feeling very randy and, seeing this, my blonde friend whips me into a neighbouring cubicle.

What happened next is all over before you can say 'Mae West'. In fact, anyone who knows the story of Mae West's three whippets will know what I'm talking about. And that was that.

But all that seems so long ago – indeed it is long ago. More recent were the times when Andy and I would go up to London – that is, if we had a five-pound note apiece – and have these terrible binges. They nearly always ended up at some ghastly place like The Bag O'Nails where any of the hostesses would go home with you if you hadn't already been separated from that fiver. When you first went into the 'Bag' the girls looked terribly unattractive, even though the lighting was very subdued. But the more drinks you had the better-looking they got – until of course you started seeing double. The trouble was that I used to get so terribly drunk, and so did Andy. I don't think there is a railing in the whole of Berkeley or Grosvenor Square that hasn't supported the two of us at one time or another: as often as not when we were both chucking up. But that, as I say, is all in the past, and a good job too.

The down behind the house at Upton has a beautiful beech-wood at the top of it. Here there is a badger's holt dug deep into the chalky sub-soil. The wood is pitted with these chalky hollows filled with dead leaves. You can lie on your back in them out of the wind and look up at the sun shining through the pale green leaves with their furry edges.

Some mornings Andy and I take the horse out. One of us rides while the other holds on to a stirrup-leather. Then we swop over. The cow-parsley is enormously high this year and often comes up to the horse's withers. The hedgerows are full of briar and convolvulus, honeysuckle and deadly nightshade. One often can find Robin's pin-cushions, which are decorative excrescences growing on the common briar, furry balls of pome-granate red. I sometimes wear them for button-holes. Andy wears oak-apples or hips-and-haws. We vie with each other as to who has the most tattered tweeds. Andy has some of his father's, who died when he was just born, but I have actually got a pair of tweed trousers belonging to my grandfather, and very nicely cut they are too.

The popular thing for the *nouveaux pauvres* to do after the Great War was to start chicken farms. This is what Andy's mother did, but it soon went bust. Now all that is left are a few old derelict chicken-houses on the slope of the hill below the beech-wood. Phoebe has taken over one of these and made it into a studio where she can paint. This is in a lovely place, half-way between the house and the beech-wood, looking right across the valley. The hut inside is rather a nice sort of mess. (It is bourgeois to be too clean and tidy, according to Phoebe.) It has been used for storing fruit, so the place smells of old apples, chicken-shit, oil paint and turpentine. I think the smell of oil paint and turpentine on freshly primed canvas is the nicest smell I know.

Phoebe lets me in there quite often nowadays and explains to me what she is trying to do. It is all to do with the French Impressionists. I find the Impressionists pretty easy to understand, particularly Cézanne. It helps, I suppose, to have been to the South of France. He absolutely captures the South of France for me and makes me long to go there again and smell the wild rosemary and the hot umbrella-pines. His colours are so clean and his brush strokes so perfectly sure. Phoebe's own work seems to be a bit of a mess but I think I see what she is getting at. At any rate she's got the theory. It worries me though that she bites her brushes all the time. After she has had a morning's chew she could equally well paint with either end. She has given me a book to read called *All Men Are Enemies*, by Richard Aldington. Phoebe says that she is going to write a psychological novel herself very soon now.

My father has just written to say 'What am I going to do?' Obviously I am a big disappointment to him. After all the Army is pretty well the last resort, and now that I've failed for that . . . he must be completely flummoxed.

★   ★   ★

Lavender's blue, dilly, dilly,
Lavender's green.
When I am King, dilly, dilly,
You shall be Queen. . . .

I can't think how it happened but Phoebe and I have become lovers. It's absolutely incredible. When you think that she is a year older than me and up at Oxford mixing with all the intellectuals . . . well, it is absolutely incredible. After all, I am only just not a schoolboy.

She smells of *Apogée* by Vionnet. We make love at every spare moment, sometimes in the chicken-house if we know Andy is up in London, sometimes in the chalk hollows in the beech-wood (though the dry leaves do stick if one is naked), but rarely in bed because of the danger of getting caught. The first time, believe it or not, we climbed into an old paper-mill just by Albert Bridge. Phoebe was a virgin. It was terribly exciting but not what you might call an unqualified success. It's laughable when you think that, of the two of us, I'm the only one with any experience – if you can call it experience. Phoebe is terrified of having a baby, and so am I of course, but one thing we are absolutely agreed upon is that French letters are indecent.

Life is very lovely, but dangerous. Phoebe's best friend, Dorkles, says she knows a sure-fire way of not having babies. She is having an affair with Rudi Vogler who is a don at Oxford. Whenever he gets into bed with her she just keeps her legs crossed. This sounds ridiculous to me. How can an Oxford don – and a professor to boot – put up with that sort of rubbish?

The Byam Shaw is an art school in Camden Street and the students are a jolly crowd, with the exception of one or two middle-aged ladies niggling away at Laocoon and Prometheus Bound in the Antique Room. Ernest Jackson, the Principal, is a nice fellow and a good academic painter, but he keeps on saying '*Courage!*' to me in French. I don't need any '*Courage!*' because I am absolutely sure I am going to become a good painter. There are several other teachers, one of whom says, 'Get it right first time.' Another one says, 'Keep a very active sketchbook.'

Occasionally I run into old school pals in London but they

really seem awfully childish now. When I say I am at an art school, they leer and talk about posing in the nude. Of course one is drawing from life every day, but I can't convince these oafs that there is nothing sexy about it. One is concentrating far too hard on what one is doing and not even the randiest student thinks about a model in any other way. Besides all my sexual energies and inclinations are reserved for Phoebe.

Talking of old school pals, Peter Allix is in the Coldstream Guards, Nigs Graham is in the Ninth Lancers and the unspeakable MacKinnon has got himself into the Black Watch. Even old Andy has gone and joined the Territorials so he is seldom down at Upton for week-ends. I only hope to God there is not going to be a war, because that would mean that Phoebe and I would be separated and that would be unbearable. She fills all my waking thoughts and living dreams. I am utterly obsessed with love for her. She, on the other hand, will not actually admit to being in love with me which mars my happiness at times. She is full of sophisticated theories about Free Love, and only living for the present. I can't live only for the present because the future has to have Phoebe in it, if only for tomorrow. But she will never make plans for tomorrow and will never even say for sure that we are going to meet but we always do – or nearly always. Most evenings we go back to my room in Limerston Street, cook some food and make love, or vice versa. Of course we are much better at it (making love) now though there is always the fear of having a baby. But sometimes she goes to Oxford for a night, or stays with her friend Dorkles, and this I don't like at all. I often wonder whether she really does stay with Dorkles. In any case anyone as attractive as Phoebe *must* attract other men. If I say anything, she gets angry and says I mustn't become neurotic. Well I don't care what you call it. The fact is that I am confoundedly jealous. But of what? Occasionally when we are at Upton a neighbouring pig-fancier who runs a model agency rings up. But though this makes me angry, nobody – absolutely nobody – could be attracted to him, even though he has got a lot of money. Phoebe doesn't give a damn about money but she is rather flattered about the modelling. He has had some professional photographs taken of her and says she is wonderfully photogenic. Of course I make fun of this (though it is true) and then we quarrel.

★   ★   ★

The most terrible thing has happened. Phoebe has gone. Gone completely. Life is a black knife in the pit of the stomach. There is no relief; only high peaks of agony. I wake up every morning and for a moment the day seems just like any other day. Then suddenly the dark shadow of remembrance engulfs me and the pain rises up again. Phoebe has gone. She is no longer here. I can no longer see her or speak to her. I can only write letters, abject cringing letters which she may not read; which she may not even get. Certainly they are not – never will be – answered. It is the end between us. This I know.

What happened was this: Tempé was 'got at', and I think I know by whom. Tempé I think – in fact, I am sure – is still very fond of me and simply accepts me as another member of the family, or did. Of course she has been aware for some time that Phoebe's and my relationship is not exactly platonic. But as long as we were all one big happy family she was perfectly content. Besides, she has been pretty busy with the 'system' now that the Flat racing season has started again. Of course, if she knew the real nature of our relationship she might be a little more concerned, but she doesn't, I'm sure. Anyway, this person has been pouring poison into her ear, saying that Phoebe mustn't be allowed to waste her time on a jobless juvenile like me. Think of all the wonderful opportunities she is missing, she says: balls, picnics and parties, trips abroad, invitations to Embassies and Vice-Regal Lodges; all that sort of thing. Well Tempé is not at all well off and it is obviously true that I am too young and too poor to make a husband. So Phoebe has gone – spirited off to Paris overnight. I can't blame Tempé. Anybody else would have done it ages ago.

The worst part is being left behind; being left where every familiar place and every familiar face is part of my life with Phoebe. One moment it is a life; a warm, throbbing, living, quarrelling, eating, drinking, fucking, sleeping, waking life. The next minute it is an oubliette, a nightmare, a tunnel without end;

52

it is wastes of grey snow under a black sky; it is the edge of the abyss: a living death.

I can't stand it. I can't put up with it. I'm not going to 'wait for three months and see how you feel'. I am active, not passive. Call me neurotic if you like but any action would be a relief from this waiting, this living in a grey vacuum, this void without end, this pain in the heart – or rather in the stomach, because that for sure is where the pain is. I must go to Paris to find her. But how? I have no money. I'll sell something, pawn something, borrow a few quid here and there. Somehow I'll raise the wind. The thing is I have *got* to get there.

★   ★   ★

This is the Hôtel du Dragon, Rue du Dragon. It is a small flop-house in a narrow street on the Left Bank. It was recommended to me by a fellow at the Byam Shaw. It is very cheap. My room, which faces on to the back, is very small and is papered in red, yellow and black triangles. Every morning a woman across the narrow well outside my window starts to laugh and laugh. After a bit one can't tell if she is laughing or crying. Then somebody starts to beat her, but she goes on laughing and crying until it all ends in screams.

I have been here for three days now. All the time I have been trying to find Phoebe. The art school she was supposed to be at has closed for the holidays. I have tried telephoning her digs God knows how many times. She is meant to be staying with a family but they keep on saying she is out – at least, I think that is what they say. My French isn't very good and it is hell trying to get through on the telephone. Nobody tries to help and everybody gets angry if one can't understand. I would do much better if I had more confidence, but the urgency of my need saps my self-assertiveness. Eventually, I pluck up enough courage to go round to her digs. A fat woman in a dressing-gown answers the bell. She looks at me suspiciously. Yes, she does know Phoebe. Is she in? No she isn't. When will she be in? She doesn't know. But she is staying there? Not now she isn't. What? Where is she then? She's not sure but she thinks she's in Berlin. BERLIN? Yes, Berlin. She went off two or three days ago with a friend. WHO?

There's no need to shout, young man. It was a friend of hers, a dark young lady with a pale skin (bloody Dorkles!). Are they coming back? She doesn't know. Now please will I stop asking questions because she has her housework to do.

I leave a note with my address and telephone number and go to the nearest bar for a pernod. For the next two or three or four days I spend my time drinking pernod and going to the cinema. The two things help to take my mind off my troubles. But they don't help all that much. Every time I take the Metro to or from a cinema, or walk in and out of a bar, I see young couples with their arms around each other, or holding hands, or kissing tenderly. This is how all young people should be, and I seem to be the only sinner in Paris all on his own.

This afternoon I get back from the cinema to be told by the *concièrge* that there is a telephone message for me. For me? How could there be? Nobody knows where I am. At this moment the telephone rings again. The *concièrge* answers it. '*Ne quittez pas,*' he mumbles surlily and, jabbing his finger at the instrument, jerks his head at me.

God knows how it happened, or how we met. It was in the middle of a street somewhere. We just rushed into each other's arms and started kissing and kissing with a crowd of delighted Parisians all laughing and cheering and egging us on. Within seconds grey, gloomy Paris became a magic city of sunny boulevards and bistros and lovers and all the corny things that the *chansons* say it is.

But that is how Paris is. We walk along the 'Boule Miche', drink a *Dubonnet au citron* and play records of Tino Rossi singing *Roses of Picardy* on the jukebox. This is how Paris really is. We go along to St Germain-des-Prés and outside the Deux Magots we see the venerable figure of Matisse. 'And that,' says Phoebe, pointing to a youngish woman by his side, 'is his mistress.' I am suitably impressed. But this is Paris. We wander through the Luxembourg and, outside the gardens, we go into the public lavatory which is men one side and women the other. Between the two is an old woman to see fair play. She is cooking *tripe á la mode de Caen* on a gas-stove and the bouquet surmounts all competition. We are enchanted. We are enchanting. We are the most lovely lovers in Paris, and Paris is the most lovely place in the world, and all mankind loves a lover.

We find another room in St Germain-des-Prés. (The Rue du Dragon has too many recent memories.) Whenever we get our breath back from making love we talk and talk. Yes, she and Dorkles had gone to Berlin to see Fritz, but it didn't work out. For one thing Fritz was working and couldn't get there, and for another the city was full of Nazis and Dorkles's friend was a Jew. So they came back. In any case André Lhote's studio is about to reopen and Phoebe wants to get back to work. I start to explain my more mature understanding of the Impressionists, but she looks at me with scorn. She is now a Fauvist, if you please. I am a little bemused by the theory, and a bit resentful too, because I am very satisfied with the Impressionists. They are right up my street. But I am not going to let that become a quarrelling point. I couldn't bear to go through that hell again, and Phoebe would leave me like a flash if I crossed her about her theories on art. So I let her assure me that all will be made clear when I meet André Lhote.

In a small back-street off the Boulevard Montparnasse is an iron staircase. At the top of it is a half-door, behind which is the sort of lavatory that consists of a large hole and two places to put your feet: in short, a squatter. This is for the convenience of the students, both male and female, of that fine ex-Cubist painter, André Lhote. Beyond is his studio, large and sunny and smelling of turps and a special sort of liquid white paint. It is big enough for a dozen or more students – of which I am now one. He is a charming man, André Lhote, and, after looking at the first painting I did there, said there could be no doubt that I had already exhibited. None of this business about 'Courage!' There's only one trouble: I think Phoebe is in a real muddle between M. Lhote's post-Cubist influence and her own theories about Fauvism. I'm not going to say anything though because we are so happy together.

At the end of each day all the students scrape the superfluous paint off their palettes with palette-knives and plaster it on the studio walls. The result is a thick and glorious multi-coloured impasto. Then, having said good night to M. Lhote, Phoebe and I go out and have a pernod or two at the café on the corner opposite the Gare de Montparnasse which, facing, west gets the full glare of the setting sun. It is the sun in my eyes as much as the alcohol that intoxicates me. When we go off to our usual restaurant I have a buzz in my head and I am walking two inches above the ground. Oh God, what a wonderful life, dipping a crust of French bread in red wine before settling down to a Chateaubriand with *haricots verts sautés*, plus a green salad with a garlic-rubbed *chapon* left in it and as much *vin ordinaire* as one can drink. This is how Paris really is in the year of Chamberlain, Munich and the Führer – the year 1939.

Today, like many Sundays, we are at Versailles. The trees are tall, cathedral-dark and silent. Sometimes at a bend in the path there is a fountain with stone seats where widows sit in their black drapes, watchful and waiting – for what? Lovers to pass by? We pass and take our picnic deep into the woods where the sun shines through the trees on to a bed of ivy. Here we eat our *baguette* stuffed with *saucisse*. There is also some Port Salut and a litre of *douze dégrées*. The wine makes me sleepy. It is so silent here. The sun, filtered through the swaying tree-tops, dapples us and the ivy leaves.

Phoebe is lying back with her eyes shut. Her skin takes on the colours of the light through the trees. The clearest green she is along her neck and under the line of her jaw. Fauve, yes. Now I understand. I lie back and look at the sun, red through my closed eyelids. Fauve. One deep breath more and I am gone, sunk into the arms of Lethe . . . Lethe?

No – Phoebe. I wake to see Phoebe bending over me, mocking. I push her off on to her back and start to undress her, button by missing button, hook by un-eyed hook. We fight a bit – she's strong – but finally she seems to win because, though naked, she gets on top of me holding me there, so that I have my rump on the ivy-bed and she her white bum in the sun.

What? – What's that? NO! it can't be! Oh my God, it really is! It is a patrol of Boy Scouts – French ones! All but the first two have seen us – and they're staring. Phoebe mustn't see – she'd never forgive me. Now I really exert my strength and hold her locked tight and kiss her, keep on kissing her, at the same time furtively glancing out of the corner of my eye. Thank God, they're disappearing now, reluctantly enough, into the woods. Yes, dammit, no – all but the last one, a mivvy little shit with spectacles who is frankly turning round and staring. He's walking backwards, damn his eyes. He'll trip if he doesn't look where he is going. I hope he breaks his neck. I am still frenziedly clasping and kissing but my manhood is going – going – gone . . . and so have the Scouts. Well, at least she will never know.

Back in Paris we find a letter from Tempé. The Territorials have been mobilized and Andy is in camp with his regiment. Phoebe must get back at once. The letter is dated 3 July 1939. It is the end of the 'good old days'. It is the end of us, too.

5

Phoebe and Peter were married in November 1939. They never saw much of each other after that. When war broke out Peter enlisted, was sent to an infantry regiment in Yorkshire for a while, and in due course was posted to an Officer Cadet Training Unit in Scotland. Eventually he was gazetted into the Rifle Brigade, at that time training on Salisbury Plain. Phoebe followed the drum a bit when and where possible, but in April, 1941, Peter was posted with a draft of reinforcements to the 1st Battalion of his regiment in the Western Desert. And that, more or less, was that. The narrative resumes.

*   *   *

Just outside Alexandria, branching off from the main road to Cairo, is a tarmac track, narrow, black and uneven, that bears off westwards between the Salt Lake of Mariut and the white strand of the sea. At this road junction is a sign-post bearing the legend 'To the Western Desert'.

In these days of waiting, I pass this notice often: sometimes in the morning on my way into Alexandria, or in the cool of the evening on my way back to camp or, occasionally, in the trembling hour of dawn when the fumes of alcohol are fading and a new sense of being replaces the intoxications of the night. At these times the idea that this road is the only one that leads to the war holds me with morbid fascination. Here in Egypt is one sort of life and down that track is another. Here is the Levant, the rich and fertile delta of the Nile, and in it a swarm of Eastern peoples. Egyptians, Arabs, Sudanese, Syrians, Mohammedans, Copts, Christians and Jews, living – or trying to live – their multifarious lives. Down there, just a few miles away in a stony desert bordered by the sea, are two northern peoples (with some reluctant Italians) intent on only one thing – making war. The only connexion between the two distinctive groups is this tenuous twist of macadam across the sand. The sign-post might as well say 'Members only' or 'Private. To the War'.

The gossip, far from encouraging, comes in from strangers passing through the camp: 'The Gazala line ought to have held' – 'The French think we let them down at Bir Hakeim' – 'Believe your 2nd Battalion had rather a rough time.' And the sporting metaphors: 'They're off in the Msus Stakes, Rommel leading the field' – 'Six-to-four Rommel, threes bar.' 'All you need,' says Jacky Wintour, 'is an iodine pencil and a pair of running shorts.'

Pat Hore-Ruthven commands our company. He and Gilbert Talbot brought back all that was left of the company: two officers and about thirty men. This is a Rest and Refit camp. Dicky Wintour (Jacky's twin), myself, and our mob of misfits are the reinforcements. 'Well, 'ere we are, sir,' said Rifleman Godfrey, 'in the land of the Pharaohs.' That Cockney good-for-nothing in his long shorts: I wonder what the Pharaohs would make of him.

Pat has given us a detail of what he calls 'Desert Manners':

(1) Never stare at individuals through binoculars. It is rude.

(2) When visiting friends, do not drive up in a cloud of dust. You will draw fire on them.

(3) When you shit, go a stone's throw away from your nearest neighbour and take a spade. If you are in any doubt as to what is a stone's throw, try crapping near an Australian.

(4) If you are invited out to dinner, take your wireless-truck and your bed-roll. Nobody will want to dig you out of a slit-trench in the dark.

(5) Do not stand on another unit's skyline. Why should they have the bother of burying you.

(6) Officers may wear what they like within reason, but steel-helmets and decorations are not de rigeur. Binoculars must be worn at all times.

(7) Before a battle be sure to make it known to whom you bequeath your liquor and kit. This will save embarrassment in the event of your demise.

(8) If you are spoken to by the Divisional Commander, do not attempt to shake him by the right hand. He hasn't got one.

Matruh has fallen. Not much further for Rommel to go. A morning's drive, no more, and still I have not smelt powder.

The sun is just up and the streets are empty except for a few *fellaheen*, their heads covered in twists of filthy cloth, sleeping on the pavements along the Corniche. Coming to the suburbs now and, as always, the egregious stink of the tannery. That smell I shall remember to my dying day. Dying day? Ho-ho! That could be tomorrow. But today is yesterday's tomorrow. Who keeps on saying that? Gilbert, is it? I know not, neither care I. But, surely, aren't these 'the good old days'?

Now we are out of the town, desert tyres singing on the sticky tarmac. Foot right down. Lovely not having a windscreen. Cools the eyeballs. Very smoky that place last night. Can still smell it on my sleeve – and that girl, what's her name? Azizza, was it? Good to be out in the fresh air, anyway. Pat's got a Besa mounted on the front of his truck. Very racy. Must try and get one for myself. Ooh, it's good to be out in the air.

*   *   *

'No. I didn't get any message.' Heart jumps, razor suspended, fingers on half-soaped chin.

'The movement order's come through. Move in half an hour,' says Gilbert.

Time to finish shaving and check my kit: one steel ammunition box (English) containing two khaki woollen shirts, one drill bush-shirt, one spare pair of whipcord trousers, pants, socks, handkerchiefs, a khaki sweater bound with leather (Indian Army issue) and a spare pair of desert boots. One ammunition box (small, English) containing shaving kit and a bottle of Après l'Ondée toilet water, one bottle of gin and one bottle of whisky. One ammunition box (small, German) containing writing paper, notebooks, *Emma*, *Ulysses*, *War and Peace*, *Charles O'Malley, the Irish Dragoon*, *Selected Poems* by Ezra Pound, T. S. Eliot, Dylan Thomas, a few coloured tins of Egyptian cigarettes, a couple of packs of cards and a roll of lavatory paper. One bed-roll containing flea-bag, poshteen coat (ankle-length sheepskin), prayer-rug from the Mouski. One bag of onions.

'Well, I'm ready.' I turn to look at Gilbert, but Gilbert has already gone.

*　　*　　*

The sun is still high when we find Henry Browne standing by himself in the middle of nowhere. The sky is very blue and the sand very yellow and he cuts a dashing figure, quite still and straight on his private patch of desert. He doesn't waste time on greetings. Maps out. Rommel has run out of petrol and the enemy have been held along the line from the Quattara Depression in the south to Ruweisat Ridge near the coast. We are digging in at Alam Halfa in the centre of the line. It is to be a 'last-man-and-last-round' operation. '*No pasarán*', and all that.

Suddenly there is a most appalling series of explosions about a hundred yards away and I swallow back something that feels like my own heart. At my other end an instinctive tightening of the sphincter just prevents me from disgracing myself. But it is only a battery of Australian 25-pounders going into action. They were there all the time, those Aussies, lurking under their scrimnets. My God! If the Aussies can shoot them, though – they can shoot us! So I must be 'up there'! At last!

It is night time, my first within range of the enemy. It passes peacefully enough save for the occasional murmur of distant guns, but I can't get to sleep. I lie in my sleeping bag by the wheel of the truck, snug enough with my feet to the wind. Sometimes I look up at the outsize desert stars, and sometimes I look at the dim forms of the soldiers lying near me. Are any of them awake too, I wonder?

The wind blows, keeping the pennons on the wireless mast astir; flick-flack, flick-flack. Finally I doze off, only to be wakened from time to time by the lulls or renewals of the far-off gun-fire, each time to see a different shade of night in the sky.

At this daybreak the sun, lightly fingering the surface of the desert, reveals Rifleman Godfrey in the enactment of a curious rite. Standing a moment in thought as if weighing the pros and cons of an esoteric problem, he moves a few paces from the truck to where a small hummock of sand has been carefully ringed about with stones. On one knee he contemplates this little mound for an instant as if in supplication. Then inserting his hand, he withdraws a can of beer from where, half buried, it has been left to cool in the dew and the night wind. Rising to his feet, he glances at the sun, and this seems to give urgency to his next move. Drawing a bayonet from its scabbard he quickly stabs two neat holes in the can and directs what he can of the gassy jet down his throat. Four, five – in six seconds the weak half-pint of near-cool, laboratory-brewed beer is consumed. He belches, losing one third of the former contents of the can. The rite is ended. Go in peace.

As the sun rises in the sky the crustaceans adhering to the person of Rifleman Venus rouse themselves and begin to deploy. The mass movement at first causes him to scratch abstractedly, then to examine himself with concern. While engrossed in this scrutiny he is surprised by a pink-faced boy called 'Mary'.

' 'ullow, Maxie,' inquires Mary. 'Wot's up?'

'Oh, go away, boy. Go 'ome to muvver,' replies Venus, returning to the search.

'Anything wrong, mate?'

'Nah, look. Piss off before I do my nut, there's a good lad.'

'All right, all right. I 'aven't said nuthink wrong. Wot's up wiv you?'

'Jus' crebs, that's all. Five akkers a dozen – and that's letting them go cheap.'

'Crabs? How d'yer mean, mate?'

'Nah look, my friend, since nobody never told yer, I was on leave in Cairo, see, and a nice gentleman comes up to me and says, " 'ullo, captain-officer, you like to buy fly-whisk?" So I says to 'im, when I want a commission and a fly-whisk I'll go and 'ave a word wiv my friend General Montgomery. So 'e says, "okay, major-corporal, special for you, I find you French gel, very white. You like it?" So I says, 'ow much? and 'e says hundred piastres, an' I say ten, an' 'e says, okay fifteen. So I 'as a bit of grumble wiv 'is dirty bint wot was as black as . . .'

'Wot yer go an' 'ave 'er for, then?' says the pink boy, sun-bleached eyebrows raised.

'Nah, look,' replies Maxie Venus in an avuncular tone. 'One day if you get out of this desert you'll want to marry some tart, see? And when yer do, yer'll be 'aving a bit of love, see, and yer'll be grinding away fit to bust but you'll 'ave been so long in the bleedin' midan that all you'll be able to manage at the end of it is a little puff of sand. So yer got to keep in practice; keep the old workin' parts clean, bright and slightly oiled. Got it? . . . Nah, go an' get yer knees brown.'

*　　　*　　　*

The sun rises and falls on the pages of *War and Peace*. The glare off the paper hurts my eyes. I lower the book and stare out across the desert where, as far as one can see, and for mile after mile beyond, are identical sand-coloured trucks in wide dispersal. Yet each truck is an island, a home round which its occupants lead their own domestic lives; a home as recognizable to its owners as any one of a hundred identical houses in a European suburb. But here in the desert the truck is the individual and man only one of its working parts. How far in time and space this is from the Russian winter of 1812. Yet is it really so far? 'There was no Sonya with whom one ought or ought not to have an understanding. . . .' Substitute Phoebe for Sonya and the situation applies. 'Here in the regiment everything was clear and simple. The whole world was divided into two unequal parts; one, our Pavlograd Regiment and the other – all the remainder.' Substitute Rifle Brigade for Pavlograd Regiment and the situation applies. Certainly, for me, to be back with the Regiment is to be back home.

South to the Quattara Depression. Dispersed in box-formation, moving over nearly a square mile of desert, our white plumes of dust rise behind us, distinguishing tank from carrier and armoured-car from truck. The desert turns white as we crunch over a million small snails nourishing themselves on the evanescent dew. By and by we pass a derelict Stuka, its silent airscrew idly turning in the wind. A drone, as of a fly in a still room, reminding us that other aircraft are not so dead, and all eyes turn skywards. A local Bofors opens up, pumping two shots a second into the clear air. Further distant, another joins in on the off-beat, thumping out a syncopated rhythm as small black explosions asterisk the sky around the indifferent plane. Half a

mile away a tank looses off a belt of Browning from its turret –
seventy-five rounds in one long stream. Catching the sun on its
silver belly like a trout foul-hooked, the Messerschmidt banks to
avoid the flack. Unharmed, it levels out and meanders off on its
way. 'Jerry Tac-R,' somebody says dismissively, and we drive on.

★　　★　　★

Night-time. As I am pulling on my sweater a figure looms up
out of the darkness and salutes. Peering close, I recognize our
Colour-Sergeant and, a little unwisely perhaps, I ask him if he
had any trouble finding us. 'Well, sir, to tell you the truth,' he
answers, 'we weren't warned till after the tanks' echelon had
gone so we had to come on our own. We followed "Sun" track
to "May" minefield and then branched off south like we had
been told, sir. We were going along quite nicely, sir, and then we
happened to meet Captain Howell-Beavis. . . .'

Oh dear, I think to myself. Obviously I shouldn't have asked.

'Yes, well, I suppose I shouldn't be giving him away, sir, but
he was stuck in soft sand so we stopped to give him a bit of a
pull-out.'

The Colour-Sergeant's white teeth grin evilly in the darkness.

'Well, sir, Captain Howell-Beavis was properly doing his nut
and said no one had told him anything – pretty good coming
from the Intelligence Officer, if you don't mind my saying so,
sir – but he was sure that you hadn't gone to "Eddie" Column
but was with the Lancers. I said I had my orders but he said *his*
orders to *me* were to go to the Lancers and if I didn't like it he'd
have me up for dripping which I thought pretty cool coming
from someone I had just pulled out of soft sand, if you'll pardon
my saying so, sir. Anyway, we followed his directions till we
passed the fallen Stuka and went on, sir, not too sure, sir, by
now – by the way, sir, Delmonte's broke a spring which took
a bit of time to change as you can imagine, sir.'

By now I was sure I had made a mistake.

'So, like I was saying, sir, by a bit of luck we ran into Captain
What-'is-name, you remember, sir, out of the Gunners, and he
said he didn't give a shit – begging your pardon, sir – what
Captain Howell-Beavis said because he'd come straight from

Brigade and heard you'd gone to join the Yeomanry with "Eddie" Column just like I'd first been told.'

'Anyway, you got here, Colour-Sergeant,' I say feebly. 'Now you'll have to take Venus back with you to report sick.'

'Got another dose, has he? I don't know, some fellows. . . .'

'Any letters?'

'No, sorry, sir, but I've got one bit of good news.'

'What's that?'

'You'll be glad to hear, sir, that our hen's come on to lay.'

* * *

'Ah, Peter,' says Colonel Eddie, giving out an effluvium of a well-known London barber's toilet preparation. 'How very nice to see you – not that I can see you very well. I think you know everybody here.'

I make a polite noise.

'Oh, perhaps you haven't met . . .' and he mentions some name which I don't quite catch. 'You may have known each other at school.'

Two tentative Old Etonians grope for each other's hands in the dark.

'What will you have, Peter? Whisky? Or some Italian wine that we seem to have come by?'

My sense of good guestmanship prompts me to opt for the Italian.

'Be honest now.'

I suppose I must have let a note of uncertainty creep into my reply because Colonel Eddie calls into the darkness, instructing someone called Fowler to bring me a glass of whisky. Meanwhile, he continues giving out orders in his own fashion.

'Are you happy about everything, Dick?'

'Yes, Colonel, but I would feel happier if "Socks" could manage one more petrol truck up with the forward echelon.'

'Socks? Where's Socks?' The colonel peers about him in the blackness.

'Here, Colonel,' comes a faintly Ulster accent.

'Do you think you can do that? I don't want to see the Light Squadron dropping out before they've gone into action.'

'Well, I could, Colonel,' comes the voice from County Down. 'But it would mean taking Timson off the water-wagon.'

'For Christ's sake, Socks,' – a spat of irritation from the Colonel – 'which is more important in an armoured battle, petrol or water?'

'Aye, guns or butter, as the marn said. Vury gud, Colonel.'

'Right, Dermot. You've got your extra petrol lorry. Sorry, Socks. . . . Now, where's that gunner? Ah, there you are. I'm sorry I've forgotten your name for the moment. You did tell me. . . . Now, you know the form, don't you? Peter Luke will be responsible for protecting your guns and both you and he will be netted in to the regimental wave-length. Oh, I do apologize, didn't anybody give you a drink? . . . Fowler!' and the shadowy cup-bearer appears on cue.

Essential business concluded, the Battle-Group Conference becomes purely a social affair with Colonel Eddie playing the relaxed host.

'By the way, Peter, how's your father?'

'I don't know I'm afraid, Colonel,' I reply. 'He's in Fiji.'

'Regular gadabout, isn't he? . . . Yes? What is it?' He bends an ear to a *sotto voce* from Fowler. 'Right, I'll come in a minute.'

Walking back towards my platoon I see the night sky to the north flicker with gun-flashes to be followed, like thunder after lightning, by the growl of distant explosions. The sound momentarily depresses me. Which is reality? Agreeable talk of friends and family, or trial by high explosive? The question once posed becomes unworthy of an answer.

Our job is to guard the leaguer at night so I make my dispositions, put on my poshteen coat and lie down just behind one of the forward sections. Soon there is silence all about. Has anyone noticed, I wonder, that the desert has no smell? That is why civilization hits one so hard in the balls when one goes back to the Delta. Scooping away some sand to fit the shape of my body, I lie and watch the Great Bear rising and at its tail Arcturus, or is it Vega? From the Pole Star I find Caseopoeia, Cephus and the Pleiades, but I get distracted and my eyes wander northwards to the gun-flashes pricking out the night-sky. I turn my back to the wind and fall asleep.

My next moment of consciousness is when a burst of Bren-fire fractures the night. As I run towards the leading section, another burst rips into the darkness at the same time as the right-hand gun joins it, making a cross-pattern of tracer in the blackness. As the echo of the last burst dies away, a single tracer-bullet, ricocheting off the stony ground, describes a leisurely arc in the sky before fading like a falling star. The echo dies away and leaves an unnatural silence in which I hear only my heavy breathing as I throw myself down on the ground.

Enemy patrol, the Corporal says. Yes. Jerries. One seemed to go down, but we'll know as soon as it's light.

Later I sleep again until once more, Bren-fire jerks me to my feet, but this time it is only the guard firing the customary three bursts to announce 'Rouse' and the dawn of a new day.

That is the pattern of our happy days; healthy days of open bowels, cool nights, ribs sprung with clean air and a sense of freedom from care that amounts to pure joy. But change of course it must, and soon.

*   *   *

'You'll never guess what I've seen,' says Oscar Howell-Beavis.

'What?' says someone.

'This will slay you.'

'Well, get on with it.'

'It's the Household Cavalry.'

'What about them for God's sake?'

'They're in PAPIÈR MACHÉ TANKS! They're all over the back-areas in old three-tonners mocked-up to look like Shermans. They'll never get over it.'

I leave Oscar telling the others about his captured Isotto Francini staff-car, whose engine he is posting home to his mother in tiny pieces, and make my way back to the platoon.

So there we are. The 'Big Push' is really about to happen. When I think about it my heart sinks, if one can so describe a sensation that takes place in the stomach. In the middle of entertaining these gloomy thoughts I hear my name called. I turn round to see the portly figure of Jim the quartermaster with his trousers round his ankles and a towel between his legs. He continues to soap his crutch as he calls out, 'How's it going, Peter-boy? Feeling a bit fed up?'

'Having a little sponge round, Jim?' I say, trying to be cheerful.

'That's right, boy. Never know when your next chance will be. Makes you feel better to know you haven't got a stuffy crutch. In the last war we never got a chance to do this sort of thing, you know.'

'I suppose not, Jim.'

'Lice and all that sort of caper we had then, boy.'

'Not too pleasant, eh?'

'No, all the same, I'll be going back to the echelon tonight when you boys get stuck in up there.'

'No more than you deserve, Jim.'

'Well, I'm a bit old for the rough stuff, now. Still I daresay it won't be too bad.'

'I must be getting along, Jim.'

'Keep your head down, Peter-boy.'

I force a smile. 'Get in all those nooks and crannies, Jim.'

The Battalion area and, indeed the whole desert as far as the eye can see, has changed within the last hour. No longer is the hundred-yards dispersion observed; on the contrary, strange vehicles, faces and cap-badges are crowding in from all sides. Near 'A' Company are some weird-looking things called Scorpions: tanks converted into a sort of threshing-machine to dispose of mines. There are sappers everywhere coiling and uncoiling – what? I don't know.

A tank regiment from another division skids into our area in a cloud of dust, making spaghetti of all the ground-laid field-telephone lines, and squats on us like a cuckoo in a sparrow's nest. Some Kiwis arrive and obdurately cook a sombre meal in silence, then continue on their way. For one hopeful moment a Mobile Bath Unit appears, pauses on tip-toe like a hunted hare, and rapidly makes off again in the general direction of Alexandria. From the opposite direction comes a scarlet-capped detachment of 'French Bob's Free Frogs' flashing weapons, smiles and gold teeth.

By afternoon everything that can be done has been done and I am able to have a little read which, if the book is good enough,

I find a very good way of taking my mind off any unpleasantness that may be in store. I'm being carried along nicely by the antics of some of Mr Evelyn Waugh's more extravagant characters, when my attention is distracted by the uncongenial sound of loud barrack-square commands being delivered in an outlandish voice.

'Starnd stull succoned fra' the luft of the reerrunk!'

I climb out from under the truck and see to my dismay a puce, sweating, bonnet-and-kilted, webbing-and-blancoed, heavily-accoutred platoon of Highlanders standing rigidly to attention.

'Oh, my God,' I think, 'this is all we need.'

Slowly, the Riflemen, in their usual state of *déshabillé*, surround them with the dumb, inert curiosity that Cockneys usually reserve for the observation of motor accidents or diggers of holes in the road.

Seeing my small black pips, this Sergeant impels himself towards me at the slope, right arm swinging shoulder-high, pack swaying grotesquely, until he pounds to a halt in a cloud of dust and a smell of sweat and webbing equipment. Smacking his butt, he reports himself regimentally: 'Sergeant Mudie, 3 Platoon, C. Company, 1st Battalion, Ross and Cromarty Highlanders – sir. Could you kindly tell us where we are?'

'Yes, Sergeant, I think so. But wouldn't you like to stand your people at ease first?'

While I ferret around in the truck for a map, Sergeant Mudie barks out the lengthy formula to enable his men to stand easy. Venus, never averse to profiting by other people's misfortunes, calls out 'What's Haitch Dee stand for?' pointing to the insignia of the Highland Division on the men's sleeves. ' 'ome Defence?' But the Jocks are either too exhausted or too polite to riposte.

At the first sign of kindliness from me Sergeant Mudie starts to unburden himself.

'We had a rendezvous with Captain Munroe at 0300 hours . . .' and he begins a confidential account of his nocturnal wanderings, ending with the touching statement that he is 'a wee bittie lost.'

I set a course for Sergeant Mudie and, once more, the poor sods hump their impedimenta and set forth into the blue with the same pathetic determination.

Gradually the platoon diminishes to an amorphous oscillation on the surface of the desert. Distantly one can hear the voice of Sergeant Mudie – 'Luft, luft, luft-ri-luft. Pick-up-the-stup-that-idle-man-there. . . . Luft – ' until it is carried away on the wind.

'That's what I call cannon-fodder,' observes Godfrey, picking with filthy fingers dead flies out of my tea.

*　　*　　*

Lieutenant Peter Luke of 'B' Company, 1st Rifle Brigade took part in the clearing of the southern part of January minefield[1] on the night of October 23/24, was there wounded and retired from the battle. This is his subsequent account of what happened that night.

*　　*　　*

The full moon was shining with great brilliance where I lay on the sand until a large fat man wearing a tin hat lowered himself down beside me so that his bottom cast me into shadow. Immediately I resented him, never having met him before, in the way that I would had he invaded my privacy in a railway carriage. All the same his presence was in one way reassuring because he had foolishly placed himself on the enemy side.

Because I was there first and because I have a sense of social obligation I opened the conversation.

'You may think it strange my lying down,' I said, 'but I have been wounded in the foot and I find it difficult to get about.'

To this he replied, without any acknowledgement of my condition: 'I'm lying down because it's a bloody sight less dangerous than standing up.'

It is important to correct at this stage any impression that I was carrying off my predicament with sang-froid. On the contrary. Things had not gone at all well for me ever since the battle had started some hours earlier. I was twenty-one years old then, and full of a romantic desire to acquit myself well. I had just read *War and Peace* – some of it by the light of the last full moon – and, in spite of the fact that I had in the last year or two discovered T. S. Eliot and Dylan Thomas for myself, I still had G. A. Henty and Rudyard Kipling in my system.

[1] Carver, *El Alamein*, 123–126.

Soon after the barrage had started, my truck had got stuck in some soft sand at the entrance to the gap in the minefield, thus isolating those who had gone before and blocking effectively the main armoured force to follow.

A carrier-load of the first wounded – a pretty gory lot, one fellow with his left leg off at the thigh and another lying on his stomach with his back ripped up – was also trying to get back through the narrow gap. If physical strength had been equal to endeavour we would have lifted our vehicle bodily out on to the hard bit of ground only a few yards away, but, though desperation had given me maniacal strength, there was nothing we could do owing to the weight of the extra machine-gun ammunition we were carrying. We had just begun to unload the truck when one of our guns taking part in the barrage started to drop them short; thenceforward for the next quarter of an hour it plopped a twenty-five pound shell at short regular intervals into our vicinity.

We had set out on the approach march in high spirits. I was certainly greatly elated and communicated it, I think, to the others. At the opening of the spectacular barrage Sergeant Jefford said, 'I'll bet that's making old Jerry shit blue lights!' and we all roared. And when this gunner behind us began laying short the men still joked, slightly hysterically, with such remarks as 'I'll tell 'is muvver abaht 'im,' and so on.

Just as we had all the ammunition on the ground, one landed within ten yards of the truck. Because it landed in the same patch of soft sand that we were stuck in, most of the shrapnel went upwards, but it was sobering and at that stage we had not properly joined battle.

At that moment Hugh, my Company Commander, appeared on foot from the gap where he had been with the leading platoon.

'What in God's name are you doing?' he said without – quite understandably – giving a thought to the convention of not bawling out an officer in front of his troops. 'You're holding up a whole Armoured Division.'

In spite of the cool night the sweat was pouring down my face and I think this concealed the tears of frustration that came into my eyes. Also my shortness of breath from exertion concealed the catch in my voice when I said, 'I'm sorry, Hugh, but I couldn't avoid the soft sand. There wasn't room.'

'I don't care. Get that bloody vehicle out of here and get up forward where you're wanted.'

His tone, it seemed to me then, implied that I had deliberately got myself stuck in order to avoid going on.

In fact, at that moment, though never thereafter, I would have rushed alone onto a Panzer Grenadier regiment. It seemed that the Scorpion designed to detonate a path through the enemy mine-field had been knocked out by an anti-tank gun and that my Vickers machine-guns were required to put this last out of action. Abandoning my truck to the crew I ran forward through the soft sand and up the narrow lane the Scorpion had ploughed until I was blowing like a tubed racehorse. The few seconds saved by this exertion would not, of course, have made the slightest differ-ence to the outcome of the battle but I was stung by Hugh's apparent unfairness.

Hugh was standing by the black and uncomfortably conspicu-ous monument of the dead Scorpion with my leading machine-gun truck behind it. A platoon on foot with some sappers was vaguely weaving about in front; beyond them was the enemy, dug-in and invisible except for irregular streams of tracer bullets that seemed to come very slowly out of the ground like the unfolding of a Japanese paper water-plant.

Hugh pointed out the muzzle-flash of the anti-tank gun as it fired again and almost instantaneously something like a very fast ball on a dry wicket bumped on the ground near the tank and bounced off into the air in a whirring long-hop.

'Get on to that bloody gun before they hit the Scorpion's petrol tank and light up the whole gap.'

'Okay, Hugh,' I said, confidence restored with the prospect of making myself, at last, effective. Jumping on to the truck next to Halsey, the driver, I told him to pull off to the left and go about a hundred yards away from the Scorpion. Hugh, in a less per-emptory tone of voice, said something about manhandling the machine-gun on account of the possibility of more mines but, because of the pandemonium of gun-fire, I waved ambiguous acknowledgement and set off with nothing now in front but the

72

moon and the occasional flash from our objective, cheerful at the prospect of vindicating myself.

The next thing seemed to be a great concussion that occurred almost simultaneously with my biting, literally, the dust. It so winded me that for a moment I could not breathe. In this condition I realized that we had gone over a mine and the knowledge of my stupidity and failure got me to my feet determined at least to make the best of a lousy job. Poor little Halsey seemed to have lost an eye but the rest of the gun-crew were just standing about repeating over and over again the invariable swear-words. In desperation I shouted the first gun-drill orders that came into my head and these seemed to take effect for the men off-loaded the Vickers and set it up a few yards away from the wrecked truck. Indicating the target, I gave a fresh order and awaited the controlled, regulated bursts and the ensuing streams of tracer which one was accustomed to expect. Nothing happened. Rifleman Schwartz, number one on the gun, was crouched over the sights with his hands in the correct manner on the firing mechanism. Thinking he hadn't heard me, I repeated the order. Again nothing happened. Schwartz sat there as still as the sentry at Pompeii. I felt like crying.

Gradually I began to understand that Schwartz was either petrified with fear or concussed by the explosion – or both. I pushed him with some difficulty away from the gun and told the corporal to take over as Number 1. Finally the Vickers hiccupped rather hesitantly into action.

Hugh suddenly appeared at my side. 'You bloody fool!' he said, in a low contemptuous tone that was quite audible in spite of the ever-increasing din of battle, and walked away again. I murmured, 'I'm terribly sorry, Hugh,' into the moon-struck, demonic void. I really meant it.

Frequently before and afterwards I had wished myself a thousand miles elsewhere in great comfort amidst sympathetic and understanding friends, but never so much as at that moment.

*   *   *

The day had started so well in the way I had come to expect from early reading of *Leatherstocking Tales*, *In Times of Peril*,

Soldiers Three and other romantic adventure stories. The sun had risen as usual on that morning of the 23rd October, which slightly surprised me as I half expected some supernatural manifestation to mark the occasion. I had dressed with some care and had taken out my oldest and nicest twill trousers from the bottom of the ammunition box which I used for clothes. They were clean and almost white from numerous washings and I put them on ceremoniously. I wore my best pair of suede desert boots and a thick woollen khaki shirt which would absorb the sweat during the day and later keep me warm at night. A silk bandana round my neck gave me the feeling of being well-dressed, and a green forage-cap which, though it gave less protection against sun than a service-dress cap, was more suitable to wear with headphones.

Having finished some *nos morituri te salutamus* despatches to various people at home, I settled down to this novel by Evelyn Waugh which had the desired effect of taking my mind off the imminence of bloodshed. Tony Palmer, a young, well-seasoned and much-wounded major who was then second-in-command of our battalion, seeing me thus composed, came across.

'Good Lord,' he said, 'how can you concentrate on reading at a time like this?' I released a smile that I hoped was both modest and serene.

That evening as the full moon rose like a rupture over the horizon the army started to move, slowly at first, starting with the smallest units and gradually gathering momentum as infantry and sappers were joined by tanks and anti-tank guns, armoured command cars, gunner OPs and a mass of such miscellaneous vehicles as made up the teeth of a mechanized striking force.

The columns, converging on the gaps in the home minefields, grew in numbers every few hundred yards so that vehicles were at times double-banked nose-to-tail, stopping, starting, grinding on in slow gear or racing forward to keep contact with those in front until the moon-bright desert seemed like the scene of some long-forgotten border-ride.

The huge moon seemed to be racing always ahead of us. Between the minefields stood two Senussi bedouin, motionles and separate in their own world, wondering but tranquil. A shout made me turn and there was Jacky Wintour alongside. It has never occurred to me since to ask him what he was doing there.

'Like trying to get to Sandown on Bank Holiday,' he shouted.

'Sandown . . . Bank Holiday,' he repeated, making tic-tac signs to emphasize his meaning.

I laughed and waved to him as he disappeared again into the throng. A tank had ground its way authoritatively between us and I looked up to see John Harding, the new divisional commander, in the turret with Robin Hastings, his G2, beside him. I stood up in my truck and saluted with brio, trying to model myself on young Rostov at the battle of Borodino. The general waved amiably, smiling. Robin, busy being *affairé*, nodded curtly and the tank, followed by its attendant armoured car, threaded its way forward.

I started to think of Phoebe and childishly wished she could see me in this dramatic setting. Then I remembered how much she despised all things military and blushed at my puerile sentiments. In the middle of these thoughts I was interrupted by the voice of Oscar Howell-Beavis who, standing lonely and dismounted as the advancing army surged past him, called out rather hopelessly, 'Have you seen the Colonel, old chap?'

'No,' I answered, 'but I've seen practically everybody else I know.'

'Oh Lord,' he said. 'I must find him.'

He stood there looking perplexed and forlorn. As we moved on he started to say something else, but his voice became drowned in the noise of grinding gears and churning tracks.

Passing with this mailed cohort through the last of our own minefields I found myself gazing with fascination at the ground which for so many weeks past had been a no-man's-land, intently scanned through glasses by day and stealthily explored by patrols at night. Because I was accustomed to the necessary dispersion of open desert in daylight and to Red Indian tactics after dark, the present City rush-hour traffic created a strong feeling of unreality.

On this strange new ground I saw another man I vaguely recognized. He had been at school with me but had altered in the intervening years. He was staring intently at his watch and, as I drew level, he looked up.

'This should be about it,' he said, as though a conversation of many years ago had never been interrupted. I was struggling to remember his name when the sky erupted with a hundred simultaneous flashes followed instantly by the pandemoniac thunder of guns. I look at my watch and noted that the battle had begun exactly on time.

* * *

I have always been amazed, in spite of much contrary experience, how any misadventure can be put right without my personal intervention. But, after being blown up on the minefield and having subsequently had the order to continue the advance, I was pleasantly surprised, being in a state of some despair, to find the rest of my platoon waiting for me. So, abandoning of necessity the crippled truck and distributing the weapons and crew round the other vehicles we went forward.

Recovering a little from the initial *Schwerpunkt*, the enemy were perking up and stuff was beginning to come back; not much artillery as yet but plenty of small-arms and thin jets of tracer were hosing round in all directions like streamers at a New Year's ball. What added to the fiesta-like quality of the evening was the pyrotechnic display of coloured Verey lights that the enemy were putting up in their frenzied desire to communicate the emergency to each other.

There seemed to be some sort of hold-up in front and now that we were through the enemy minefield our people had spread out into a semi-circular bridge-head. I therefore had a few moments of leisure in which to indulge in my favourite occupation of gazing about me and letting my mind wander. Assuming that to every one tracer bullet there were at least three invisible ones I was beginning to wonder what sort of pattern, if the courses could be plotted, all these bullets were making round *me* personally when Bill Jepson-Turner, who was second-in-command of our Company, came up and told me to get the machine-guns into action and to engage an area where a lot of enemy fire was coming from.

This seemed to be exactly the job for us.

'Good, Bill! Fine!' I said. 'Right-ho! Okay!' And in a few minutes all four guns were sweetly pumping lead into the desert with drill precision. I began to feel better and went from gun to gun saying encouraging things like: 'Well done, so-and-so! Keep at it! Nice easy traversing, now. Sights up a bit. That's the stuff!' and all the usual guff. I began to think all might be forgiven but I was too optimistic. Hugh rushed up.

'For Chrissake cease fire!' he shouted. 'You're firing right into our leading platoon. Mulford's been badly hit.'

'But, Hugh . . .' I said, deflated at once. But he went on: 'What the hell did you open fire for anyway?'

Quite suddenly I lost my temper.

'I was *ordered* to engage that bloody target,' I shouted, turning round to face Hugh, but he had already disappeared.

I went off to find Bill and vent my grievance. Bill was – and still is – a well-built fellow and very calm, but he was upset about Mulford. Bradbury and Mulford were the two best sergeants in the Company. Of heroic stature, they were both young, handsome, of splendid physique, dead shots, intrepid and full of initiative. One, if not both, had already been decorated by that time. Apart from personal feelings, therefore, it was not unnatural that Bill, who had great concern for the men, should have been upset.

We were walking along together; he was a few paces in front and the moon was so bright that I noticed a small boil on the back of his neck. Bill had a low and what is sometimes described as well-modulated voice but suddenly he let out a silly, feminine little 'Ow!' and fell down.

'Are you all right, Bill?' I asked rather stupidly, and the next second my leg received what felt like a hard knock from a heavy stick so that I too fell down. Bill started to shout for Hugh, calling out that he had been hit.

'I've been hit too, Bill,' I said. But he didn't take any notice.

Some minutes later Hugh came up and got some fellows to cart Bill away. They didn't come back for me but eventually Bonning, my driver, came over with my tin hat and advised me to put it on. I apologized for causing him the trouble and explained that I had been wounded. He said, 'You've got dead lucky, you have. There's a bullet-hole right through the back of your seat in the truck.'

77

He squatted down whilst we chatted for a moment. I told him to share out my liquor and tinned fruit amongst the others and then sent him back to tell Sergeant Jefford to take over the platoon. That was the last I ever heard of Bonning except for a nice letter received later in hospital.

*   *   *

And that was how I came to be lying beside the fat man on the sand in the moonlight.

The fat man took the opportunity of a comparative lull in hostilities to get his huge bulk perpendicular and went away, leaving me feeling very exposed. I therefore tried to get up and found that I could hop without much pain (I hadn't been feeling very much in any case), so I hopped in stages over to Company Headquarters' truck where I found Corporal Bower and his mate extremely busy on the two wireless sets. I admired very much the detachment with which they concentrated on maintaining communications, sitting as they were completely unprotected and high above the ground.

After a while Hugh came back. 'Look,' he said, 'there's a truck going back with wounded. You'd better get on it . . . and looked after Mulford. He's very bad.' So I got on to the back of the truck and made myself as comfortable as possible. Then Mulford was handed up to me and I got him in the best position possible which was in my arms with his head against my shoulder as if I were spooning with a girl. In this way I could cushion him a bit against the bumps. He seemed quite unconscious but murmured a bit from time to time.

We started back over the uneven ground. The driver was a good little chap who later became a sergeant but he lost his way, for which he could hardly be blamed, and I could not navigate owing to my position and having poor Mulford in my arms. I was getting rather worried about him because he soon stopped murmuring and so I started swearing at the driver, who, though lost, was doing his best to get us back to the Casualty Clearing Station. I suppose I was beginning to suffer from shock myself and each time we lurched over some particularly bad ground I cursed rather hysterically at the driver. I saw him often later on

78

in the war but he never alluded to the occasion nor appeared to bear any resentment.

The moon was going down when we reached the Casualty Clearing Station. My first impression of it was that it was very little different from the one to which Prince Andrey was taken after the battle of Borodino except for the availability of morphine, sulphanilamide and the saline drip. There was a tent or two surrounded by men on stretchers variously wounded, and a number of doctors and orderlies moving about with an air of urgency. A few long-range but heavy enemy shells were lobbing over so that the medical staff were working under duress. It was my impression then, and subsequent experience confirmed it, that the nearer they were to the front line the better the medical profession behaved.

A doctor and some orderlies came over to the truck. I explained about Mulford and handed him gently down and they laid him on a stretcher. The MO went over him perfunctorily and then turned to me with a funny look in his eye.

'What did you want to bring him all the way back here for?' he said. 'He's been dead some time.'

This was a shock. I had made several attempts to take Mulford's pulse but it had been impossible because of the bouncing of the truck, so I had just held him as still as possible. So Mulford was dead and I was sorry, but somehow I'd guessed it anyway. What really upset me now was the implication (for the second time in one night) that I had invented an excuse to get away from the battle.

He was still looking at me, very straight in the face, as all these thoughts and attendant emotions raced through my head. 'I don't think I need detain you any longer,' he said.

'Oh, but . . .' I said with the sudden pleasant realization that I was about to play a small trump card, 'I've been wounded too.'

The MO's face gave a slight start of guilt which was all that I required of him.

'Oh . . . have you?' he said. Then, after a momentary pause, 'Well, hop off then.' And he gave me a hand down.

But the miseries of the night were not yet over. The stretcher-bearers carried me over and put me down amongst others lying outside the tents. Two stretchers away was a man with plasma tubed into his leg from a bottle attached to a tent-rope. He had been badly wounded in the groin and he moved his head regularly from side to side, sometimes raising it to try and have a look at the fearful damage done to himself. But this last effort was mercifully beyond him and his head fell back and again started to move rhythmically from side to side. Although untouched about the upper part of his body, his appearance had altered so strangely that I watched him for some time before I realized that it was Sergeant Bradbury. I shot upright on the stretcher.

'Sergeant Bradbury!' I said, 'Bradbury! It's me. . . .'

But he never answered or showed any sign of recognition. Nor, I gathered, did he ever speak again. So Bradbury and Mulford, the two who had seemed most indestructible, both died in the same night.

Somebody then quite unnecessarily stuck a shot of morphia into me and eventually I was put into an ambulance which rumbled off into the night.

Soon the sound of gun-fire receded and a pleasant drowsiness came over me and I allowed myself to imagine I was in a *wagon-lit* going to Alt-Aussee in the Saltzkammergut for the summer.

I played this game with myself for a while and listened in my mind's ear to the sounds of European railway stations at night; to the sounds of girls calling '*Chocolade-cigaretten-mineralwasser*' on the platform, until I was gradually prised out of my soft drugged dream by another noise of someone very close and in great pain cursing violently but distinctly. I was brought back to my senses by this agonized voice which was enraged to the point of being tearful. Above all it was a voice that I thought I knew. . . . I could see quite well in spite of the darkness inside the ambulance and a figure, his whole head and face shrouded in bandages, was slowly waving his bound arm in the air.

'Is there anything I can do?' I asked him.

'Get them to stop. Get them to stop,' was all that he would say.

I realized that he had been burned – in a tank presumably – and that there was probably not much point in my stopping the ambulance but with some difficulty I did so all the same. They gave him a shot of morphia and we went on.

The familiarity of the voice worried me. He was obviously an officer in one of our armoured regiments and he might easily have been a friend. Was he the man Colonel Eddie introduced me to in the dark? Was it the man looking at his watch at the gap in the minefield?

'Who are you?' I asked. But all he would say was, 'I wish to Christ they would stop.' Gradually the morphine took effect and he quietened down. I never found out who he was.

Some time during that interminable night we arrived somewhere. That is to say we were taken out of the ambulance and carried on our stretchers to a tent.

'Where are we?' I asked.

'El Alamein,' was the reply.

'Let a *Te Deum* be sung,' I said.

'What's that?'

'Nothing.'

'Lousee Pommee baastard!' came an unmistakable accent out of the darkness.

After that I went to sleep more or less, but my mind was such a vortex of conflicting emotions in which fear, elation, mortification, relief, anger, happiness and sorrow, to mention some of the less complicated ones, were all jostled together, that to call it sleep was an over-simplification. Eventually, however, I must have gone off because my next conscious realization was of being in a big tent with bright sunshine outside and a doctor going from stretcher to stretcher.

As I lay there letting the flood of recent memory return a Church of England padre came into the tent. He was shaved and, for an excusably un-military figure, looked quite spruce. He also gave an impression of one who had recently had quite a good breakfast and a satisfactory evacuation. He walked in rubbing his hands crisply together.

'Any dead?' he called over to the MO in a cheerful voice. 'Any dead? Any dead?'

6

The stink of the Port Tewfik oil refinery blows across on the prevailing wind and makes me want to vomit, but vomit I cannot. All I can do is to hobble from time to time to the outdoor latrine and urinate a dark liquid the colour – with respect – of Guinness's stout. Sometimes I manage to excrete some matter whiter than anything ever defecated by a spoilt Aberdeen terrier on a London pavement. The whole operation, plus the smell of the creosote with which the latrine had been painted, makes me want to puke, but puke I cannot. I can only sing under my breath:

'*King Farouk, King Farouk,*
Hang your bollocks on a hook!'

I have the yellow jaundice and I'm lying here with my mind drifting like an empty boat in a heavy swell, feeling too sick to read, to write, to talk, or even to think except in inconsequential snatches.

I remember at the Club Royale de Chasse et de Pêche seeing someone squirt King Farouk with a soda-water syphon, and I remember the King laughing and inviting the fellow to have a drink. He loved that sort of thing; reminded him of his Sandhurst days, I suppose.

'*He's the King of the wogs,*
The jackals and the dogs,
Quoiss ketir mangaria
Up your pipe bardin'.'

I remember many things lying here. I remember Sorbo, our White Russian officer, complaining about another officer from the Regiment who had recently joined Divisional Staff: 'Noel now he at Div got too swollen for his shoes, but I tell him he just a squeak-pip officer.' That same night Sorbo went out on patrol and in the dark fell into an Italian latrine-pit. Noel told him the next morning, when he went to report direct to the General, that it was nice to see him looking so shit-shape.

> 'Queen Farida give me buckshees,
> Queen Farida give me buckshees,
> She's the Queen of the wogs
> The jackals and the dogs. . . .'

I remember Mark trying to buy a thirteen-year-old Senussi bint from her father – it was somewhere near El Mreir, I think. The bargaining went on for hours; a few tea-leaves here, a few grains of sugar there, being added bit by bit to the marriage-price. Eventually the Bedouin got up to go. The deal was off. '*Mafeesh shai*,' he said quite simply – 'Not enough tea.'

> 'She's the Queen of the wogs
> The jackals and the dogs,
> Shufti Koos, Mafeesh faloos
> Quoiss bint, bardin'.'

I remember having the old dysentery. (A far cry from what is happening to me now.) On the march my truck had to drive like hell up to the front of the Column so that I could get out, squat, and squitter while the whole battle-group drove past. By the time we got back to our proper place we very often had to do the whole manœuvre all over again. Sometimes they would barrack and then the lads on my truck would either shout back loyally or hide their faces in shame. Eventually, I got so bad that I was sent back to 'B' Echelon where John Freeman (he was called 'Red' Freeman then. Nothing to do with politics – just the colour of his hair), kindly fixed me up with a latrine of my own made out of petrol tins and had it placed handy to my bed so that I could stagger from the one to the other and, of course, back again.

One bright morning I was sitting on the can, sweating and shivering at the same time, when a staff car drove past about fifty yards away. The occupant was a superior-looking Guardee who seemed to be signalling at me. As he passed he glared at me with a look of impotent fury on his face. He was still glaring when a series of trucks and cars containing Military Police, Provost-Marshals and other unfamiliar officials drove by and they too stared malevolently. I had just begun to realize that some unusual event was taking place when a very grand staff car with a Union Jack on its bonnet almost ran me down. In it I had no difficulty in recognizing Generals Alexander and Montgomery. Between them was a rotund figure in dungarees topped off by an old-fashioned topee. I was of course in a serious dilemma, glued like that to the can, but on reflection, since I was not wearing a cap, I think I did the right thing: I sat stiffly to attention and gave a smart eyes-right. Winston Churchill removed the cigar from his mouth and extended it towards me between two fingers in a benign salute.

★ ★ ★

I remember the first night of the battle of Alam Halfa. Robin Hastings put his boot into my ribs as I lay sleeping and said, 'Get up. There's a full-scale attack all along the line.'

The next night I was alone in the ACV[1] with Mike Carver[2] and Robin Hastings. Carver was only a Lieutenant-Colonel then and about twenty-six years old. He was tall and pale and very relaxed. He sat with his legs stretched out, earphones round his neck, watching in a detached manner the situation map on the wall. It had been a long day since three o'clock in the morning and all the time the Division had been pulling back while inflicting maximum damage to the enemy. This was all according to plan. Mike Carver yawned and said, 'Thank God the General's gone to bed. He makes me feel like a mid-wife at a first confinement.' Robin neatly chalked up a new position on the map with a chinograph pencil. 'Eddie Column in contact just west of May minefield. Some open-sight fire from 88-millimetres. About four zero MET[3] moving sou'west,' he reported.

'They've got them up quick. Who did you say that was?'

'Eddie.'

'Good . . . thanks.'

[1] Armoured Command Vehicle.
[2] Later General Sir Michael Carver, GCB. Became Chief of General Staff in 1971.
[3] Mechanized Enemy Transport.

Carver lowered himself as horizontally as possible in his swivel-chair and closed his eyes.

Presently there was a loud knocking on the ACV door. Robin went to open it.

'Yes?' he said, in his most forbidding manner.

In the light of a distant parachute-flare I could see a young officer of the 60th – one of the Wake brothers I think it was – and behind him darkly a truck.

The subaltern spoke up politely.

'Could you possibly tell me where the nearest MO is? I've got some wounded here.'

'The CCS[1] is five hundred yards to the north-east.'

'Could you possibly show me exactly where . . . we've been swanning around for over an hour. . . .'

'Look here. This is the Divisional Commander's Ack One. You'll have to find it yourself.'

A note of humble desperation came into the other's voice. 'There's a man here with his leg off. I must get. . . .'

'I can't help that. You'll find it if you keep on.'

Robin turned back leaving me to close the door. As the truck started up again I heard a man in the back cursing and blaspheming viciously. And then I heard the voice of the subaltern shrill with misery and impotence.

'For Christ's sake shut up that effing and blinding. We're in Divisional Headquarters.'

I closed the door on the painful scene.

*　　*　　*

I remember not long afterwards 'French Bob' coming excitedly into the General's Mess, gold teeth flashing in the sunlight. 'We've been cut to pieces,' he said happily, and it was no great exaggeration. I offered him a consoling gin.

'Shin-shin, ol' boy,' he said raising his glass in a toast.

*　　*　　*

I remember one day stopping to look at some graves, the usual

[1] Casualty Clearing Station.

85

mounds of sand with a tin hat or a rough wooden cross on top.
One of them bore the inscription –

No. 759083. Sgt. Mudie J.
2nd Bn Ross & Cromarty Highlanders

*　　*　　*

It was nothing very important, just an Italian rearguard that's all.
We were in reserve and I had nothing better to do than to
wander down into the valley to pick some wild flowers and see
how they were getting on. I can't remember who it was I was
chatting to all the time. There were a few mortar bombs coming
back but nothing really to bother about. The next thing I remember noticing was a stretcher coming towards us with somebody
on it whom I did not recognize. I stared at the man on the
stretcher thinking that he looked vaguely like Geoffrey Fletcher –
then with a shock I realized that it *was* Geoffrey Fletcher and that
he was smiling at me. I spoke his name I think, but no answer
came back because by now I could see that his tongue had been
stitched to his upper lip to stop him swallowing it. As the stretcher
bearers stopped for a few seconds' rest Geoffrey went on smiling
at me and I went on staring at him stupidly. He then raised something under the blanket so that the blanket fell off. What he was
raising was the stump of his leg severed clean off at the calf.

Just after Geoffrey had been taken away, half a dozen Italian
prisoners came down the hill with their hands up. They were all
shouting excitedly and the first one to see that I was an officer
rushed up to me shouting and spitting in my face that somebody
had pinched his wrist-watch. I had a pair of ammunition boots
on that day and I kicked him as hard as I could up the arse.

*　　*　　*

The stench of that oil refinery. . . . Last night a fellow opposite
died of hiccups. We knew he was dead because at about 0300
hours the hiccups stopped and this morning the usual old
screen was put round the bed until he was lugged off.

There is a radio in the ward here and it is playing a regimental
march. It reminds me suddenly of dear old bloody Tidworth the

day we left for the Middle East. It was six o'clock of a cold and frosty morning, and Mr West with the Regimental Band was there to march us to the station and play us off. But it was freezing so hard that, between stuck valves and cracked lips, not a note could the bandsmen get out of the brass till we were half-way up the hill. That seems an awful long time ago. I was only twenty then, and now I am twenty-two.

* * *

Soon after the fall of Tunis in May 1943 Lieutenant Peter Luke was promoted Captain, but within a few weeks he was (quite properly) broken for an extra-regimental misdemeanour which came to the ears of the new Commanding Officer, Lieut-Colonel Victor Paley. That September the 7th Armoured Division,[1] which included 1st Rifle Brigade, landed at Salerno in Italy and shortly afterwards, his peccadillo purged, Luke's captaincy was restored to him. The narrative resumes:

* * *

Nobody who has not just spent a year in a desert; who has not come from that desert to the *campagna* of Naples in the soft sun-shine of September can know what the word Autumn means – not even if he has read Keats's poem. Everything that is ripe and good is here for the asking. Clean water is here to bathe in, to wash in, to drink. Tomatoes are here for the picking; round red ones and little yellow pear-shaped ones, the sweetest of all. There are persimmons large and opulently yellow, green walnuts that peel white as teeth, grapes in extravagant abundance and never one grudged by the peasants who grew them. Only girls are not quite so easily to be had, although there are opportunities. (Hearing loud squeals the other day from a house in Aversa, I went into a room where I found two of our gallant sergeants holding a naked whore upside down by the legs. I don't know exactly what was happening but it was a cheerful scene.)

As I say, only those with puckered desert eyes, like the men standing beside me now looking across this vine-and-olive-terraced valley, can know the full meaning of the word Autumn.

[1] The Divisional insignia was a jerboa which gave rise to the popular newspaper cognomen, 'The Desert Rats'.

But do not be deceived. Do not be deceived because death is everywhere. Death is at every bridge and every cross-roads marked on a German map. Death is in every golden vineyard concealing in its bounty lethal German S-mines. Death is in every ochre villa set temptingly among tall cypress trees, with its lavatories booby-trapped to explode in the arse of the ignorant desert soldier. Death is in the flooded melon-fields, where German dead lie soft-lapped in water gently soaking flesh from bone. Death, with its sweet stench, is in the ditches where blow-flies swarm in the stomachs of sun-dried men. But death is worst of all in the white villages where the senseless poor in their impotent panic rush out into the streets as the bombs and shells fall: bombs and shells dropped impartially by old friends, now enemies, and old enemies, now friends. Perhaps it is the very ripeness, the *pourriture noble*, of death that makes all here so painfully and exquisitely beautiful.

★   ★   ★

Rifleman Sidney Kitchener Mons Borley (son of an Old Contemptible) is in trouble. It started when Corporal Maggs's section was warned for the patrol. Borley, it should be mentioned, is Maggs's mate.

'I'm not going, Maggy,' he said, very calm and quiet. Maggs didn't quite get the drift. 'Come again, mate,' he said.

'I said I'm not going, mate, that's all.'

'That's what I thought you said the first time,' said Maggs.

'Well, that's it then, isn't it?'

'What's the matter with you?' said Maggs, still not quite catching on. 'Feeling queer or summink?'

'No. Like I said, I'm not going.'

'Who said?'

'I did.'

'You went last time.'

'I know I did, but I'm not going this time.'

Poor Maggs was in a state. It was Borley who remained calm. And of course the matter had to come up in front of the Company Commander.

At first Bill was a bit sharp and peevish but he quickly saw that we were facing a serious problem.

'I really don't understand you, Borley,' Bill said. 'It is your section's turn for the patrol. All your mates are going. You've always been before.'

Borley was being very brave, really, sticking to his guns, but I could see he was deeply upset.

'It's just that I've decided against it, sir.'

'Decided against what, Borley?'

'Against going, sir,' his lip quivered a little. Bill began to get exasperated.

'I know that. You've said it before. What I am asking is on what grounds you are refusing to go on patrol with your section?'

'Well, sir, I've decided against. . . .' He paused for a second, then blurted out: 'I don't think it's right, sir.'

Bill was stumped. We all were. There was a long silence while Bill decided what to do. I could see he was trying to be fair yet there was confusion in his mind. In this sort of situation his own sense of right and wrong was not complicated by vain philosophies.

'Now, Borley, understand this,' Bill said. 'Refusal to take part in a patrol against the enemy is a Court Martial offence equivalent to desertion or mutiny. In other words, it's about the most serious offence there is. Do you fully understand that?'

'Yes, sir, I realize that.'

Bill turned to 'Birdie' Wren, the Company Sergeant-Major.

'Sergeant-Major, have you had any previous trouble of this sort from Rifleman Borley?'

'No, sir,' said Wren. 'He's always gone along with the lads – I mean he's always been a good clean soldier, sir.'

Bill turns once more to Borley. 'Well, I'm sorry, Borley, but I shall have to put you under close arrest. You'll be up for Commanding Officer's Orders as soon as we're out of the line.' Then to the Sergeant-Major, 'Meanwhile, Sergeant-Major you will arrange a prisoner's escort.'

For a moment there was silence. Birdie Wren looked embarrassed. Then he took a pace forward and murmured something in Bill's ear.

'All right then,' said Bill to Borley. 'Consider yourself under close arrest but report back to your section till further orders.'

The problem is, of course, that we are hopelessly under-strength. Though we have not been engaged in any major battle, there has been a constant trickle of casualties; for example at Aversa, at Afragola, at Cardito and on the banks of the Volturno. We certainly cannot spare men for Prisoner's Escort. But neither Bill nor I, lacking regular soldiers' knowledge of King's Regulations and the Manual of Military Law, know exactly how a case of refusal to go into action should be treated. A message is therefore sent to the Adjutant and in due course Dick pitches up in our lines. But he has no solution either. The Colonel is much too busy to hold Orderly Room and he, Dick, is not prepared to recommend that Borley should be sent back to 'B' Echelon.

'Why,' he says, 'should a man who is virtually a deserter enjoy the comparative safety and comfort of the echelon?'

'Because,' argues Bill, 'it is bad for morale to have a man like that up in the front line setting a bad example.'

'Can't help that,' says Dick, 'you'll bloody well have to keep him till I've had a chance to talk to the Colonel.'

'Did you see the duck this morning?' asks Dick as talk turns to other things. It appears that he brought a 12-bore out from England and has had the luck to have preserved it intact ever since. Bill and I only have two old hammer affairs which we scrounged from the town hall at Aversa. 'That's better than nothing,' says Dick, 'why don't we have a crack tomorrow morning?'

Meanwhile, on a grassy bank behind some tall bamboos where the Section is preparing for the night patrol, Corporal Maggs is trying to get at the reason for Borley's astonishing decision. Borley himself seems willing enough to talk but what he has to say does more to confuse than enlighten. Apparently yesterday Maggs had let Borley, equipped with the Section's chocolate and cigarette ration, go off on the scrounge. He had not had too much luck. In the first instance he had met an old farmer who had given him a dozen eggs in exchange for a packet of fags. They had just shaken hands on the deal when a Messerschmidt on a ground-straffing dive had sprayed the whole area down with a burst from its machine-guns. When they had picked themselves out of the cow-dung the old man was amused to find that his English cigarette was still alight, while all but one of Borley's eggs were broken.

'The old bleeder's still laughing, I wouldn't wonder.'

'All right, Sid,' says Maggs, 'so you bust a dozen eggs.'

'Eleven.'

'Eleven then, but it weren't your fault. Nobody's blaming you, are they?'

'I haven't said they was, have I?'

'Well then?'

But Borley still has a lot more to say. The next farm he came to was a poor-looking place but there was a girl outside it feeding some hens. She was a lovely girl according to Borley. She had bare brown legs and wore a plain black dress. She had nodded and smiled at him in a very friendly way and went on feeding the chickens. When she bent over to give them some water he could see her beautiful olive thighs, he said.

'You know how some of these Eye-tie tarts aren't 'arf hairy. Well this one's legs were kind of smooth, like – '

'Eggs?'

'That's right, mate, but natural. And she had a pair of Manchesters – you could tell she weren't wearing nothink under.'

He had then produced chocolate and the odd tin of food by way of barter and she had looked at him full of warmth and gratitude. He pointed once more at the hens but she didn't seem to understand and beckoned him towards the house, smiling all the time.

'I couldn't believe it, mate. All the time she was giving me the come-on and feeling me all over for more of them what's-its. She got her hand in my trouser pocket once. Cor! I thought she'd notice I was getting a hard on.' And all the time he was getting closer to the house. ' "Chicken," I said, "chicken . . . cock-a-doodle-doo," but she'd got a grip on my arm like a rozzer on a Saturday night. When we got to the house it was all dark inside and ever so quiet. "You're going to get lucky, Sid," I said to myself, "You're going to get lucky." '

'She went in first and I could just imagine that little cotton frock coming off like the wrapper off a Mars Bar. I went in after her. All black it was; I couldn't see nuthink. I heard her laugh so I put out my hands to give her a squeeze. I don't know what I got hold of but I can tell you, mate, I dropped it pretty sharpish. I think it was the kisser of an old woman wivout any teef. Then I began to see. I could see the room was crammed with them – old bags with no teef all dressed in black sitting round in a circle. I couldn't see no sign of my bint nowhere.

'All of a sudden one of the old bags let out a terrible yell. I think she was laughing. Then all the others joined in at the tops of their bleedin' old voices, yacking and cackling away fit to bust, and I could see they were cramming their bleeding gobs with the chocolate ration and screaming all at the same time.

'Well I tell you, mate, I never seen the old zubrick go down quicker. I legged it for the door then, but I tripped over a chicken and bust the last of the eggs.'

'Well, you dropped a bit of a sconer, mate, losing all the lads' rations,' says Maggs, 'but that's no reason for wanting to jag it in.'

'I hadn't lost all the lads' rations. There was one bar of chocolate left and that's what I'm coming to.'

Sneaking back to the Battalion area by a devious route in order not to be seen, he came to an uncleared German minefield marked with the usual skull and cross-bones and the sign 'ACHTUNG! MINEN!' Wondering how to get round it, he noticed that the wire was down on the far side where a shell had exploded. At that moment he saw coming towards him from the other side of this gap two little Italian children, brother and sister, walking hand in hand. The elder, a boy, appeared to be about seven and the little girl a year or two younger.

'You know what it's like with them Eye-tie kids, Maggy. A British squaddy just means one thing – chocolate. And that's how it was, mate. Soon as they saw me they started yelling their bleedin' heads off, "*Inglesi – carameli, Inglesi – carameli*," and started running towards the gap in the wire.

'Christ, mate! I didn't know what the fuck to do. The more I started shouting "Get back" the more they thought it was all part of the game; and then it happened. You know what it's like with those bleedin' S-mines, they go straight up, like Captain Fletcher's leg. It was the little girl got it. One moment she was holding her brother's hand, the next moment she wasn't there. There wasn't no bits even – nothink. Just some little gobs of blood in the other one's hair like. He didn't even seem to notice – just stood there not crying nor nothink.

'Well I tell you, mate, I did something I'll never do again in my life. I was over that wire and across the minefield in a flash – never even looked to see where the fuckers were. I just picked the poor little bugger up jilty and flung him back through the gap.'

'What happened then, Sid?'

'Well, I suppose they must have heard the bang because a whole lot of Eye-ties came up screaming and yelling and when they couldn't see the little girl they started going raving mad. I think they thought it was my fault.'

'What you done then?'

'Just slung the little bloke the last bar of chocolate and scarpered.'

*　　*　　*

Life is always a bit tense at Company Headquarters till a patrol comes back. I sit trying (in vain) to make the imprest account balance while Bill stalks about morosely chewing the inside of his cheek. To make the situation even gloomier we have Rifleman Borley with us since it is his section out on patrol. Only Birdie Wren makes any attempt to keep things cheerful by elaborating some rumour that the Division will be home for Christmas – all except for those with VD.

Just before midnight there is a slight commotion in the dark and the sodden figure of Acting-Corporal Parry appears, stinking of marsh-water. He goes up to Bill and unslings his rifle without even giving it a tap.[1]

Over in Corporal Maggs's section area Birdie Wren is dishing out tea and a rum ration to the others back from the patrol. The men queue up silently and then seek out their bed-rolls before taking off their dripping equipment and mud-soaked clothes. Borley is helping the Sergeant-Major dish out the rum and hot

[1] 'Tapping the sling' is the Greenjacket form of salute when carrying a rifle.

tea but nobody seems to acknowledge his presence. Eventually the silence becomes too much for him.

'Where's Maggy?' he asks. 'Where's Corporal Maggs?'

But there is no sound except for that of equipment being thrown sullenly down and the squelch of sodden boots being sucked from wet feet. Borley hands a mug of tea to Rifleman Miller who takes it in silence.

'What's up, Dusty? Where's Maggy then?'

'Dunno,' comes the reply, and the man turns away.

Taylor comes next, a tall thin fellow with a full set of false teeth.

'Slim? Where's Maggy?'

Slim Taylor slurps some hot tea through his dentures. 'Why ask me?' and he sucks in more tea with hollow cheeks.

' 'ere, Ginge, turn it up, will you,' he says grabbing a third soldier by his webbing-equipment. 'Where's Maggy? Where's Corporal Maggs? . . . He's my mate you know.'

'Was, you mean.'

'What do you mean, was?'

'Well he's not 'ere, is 'e?' says the man called Ginger.

'Where the fuck is he then?'

'Why should you worry?' says Ginger. 'You're all right Jack, aren't you?'

Borley turns round addressing the section in general.

'What's the bleeding secret? Why don't you tell me where Maggy is?'

At that moment Bill appears and approaches Birdie Wren.

'Sergeant-Major, message from C Company. Corporal Maggs's body has been picked up. Their forward platoon found it floating downstream. Send a stretcher first thing, will you.'

Instinctively I look round at Borley. He is standing as if he were facing a firing-squad. But he's not facing anybody because the rest of the section have turned their backs. They are very busy getting off their wet kit.

* * *

It is stand-to, and not yet first light. Dick appears as I am putting on my gum-boots. I can just make out his elegant figure but there's something strangely unfamiliar about it and it takes me a moment to realize what it is. Instead of carrying a stick or a revolver he has a shot-gun under his arm. Further off I can hear Bill talking to somebody about the assault-boat, a collapsible canvas affair. Dick passes me his flask which has whisky in it and I take a grateful swig. The Sergeant-Major appears to report the Company stood-to. He also accepts a pull from the flask.

As dawn breaks we can just discern the mile-wide estuary of the Garigliano whose fens, marshes and callows are intersected here and there with dykes and causeways. It is this watery delta that forms the 'no-man's-land' between us and the Germans dug into the high hills beyond.

Bill, having warned the forward platoons of our intention to move out beyond their defensive positions into the water-meadows, now joins us and suggests we make a start before it gets too light. But first the Sergeant-Major has something to say: what, he asks, are we to do with Borley?

'Christ,' says Bill, and for a moment there is a leaden silence.

'I should have thought the answer was perfectly simple,' says Dick. 'We take him with us.' And then as an afterthought. 'He can man the assault-boat.'

Within half an hour the three of us are in position, spread out on a semi-circular causeway between a small lake on the one hand and a water-meadow on the other. The wind is blowing nicely off the sea and visibility is just good enough.

Dick fires a shot in the air and at once the thrilling sound begins; a whirring whickering at first, followed by the sound of thousands upon thousands of wings beating first the water and then the air. To begin with we see mainly teal, but the light, quickly improving, soon reveals widgeon, sheld-duck and a number of pintail. Flighting up into the wind, the birds circle again and again over the causeway so that all three guns are firing as fast as they can load. Dick with his own 12-bore does the best, but Bill is managing pretty well too. Even I, though I am a bad shot except with a rifle, quickly get about seven birds in as many minutes.

It is a wildfowler's paradise, but soon many more birds are dropping into the water than we can possibly retrieve and, though Borley is doing his best in the assault boat, the absence of gun-dogs is badly felt.

Physically Borley is a weed, and not a very well-grown one either. He has a pale pitted skin and his comportment is such that on anything like parade or inspection he always gets stuffed in the rear rank. On the other hand he is usually cheerful and has some elements of the Cockney sparrow about him which makes him easy to live with. However, what we have been seeing for the last twelve hours or so, is a new Borley, both mystifying and upsetting. It's too easy to dismiss a man by saying that he has been 'up the Bluey' too long. It is not as simple as that because it takes guts to stand up to Bill when he puts on his Company Office voice, and Borley has stood up to him. But last night Borley looked stricken, and this morning there is something frenzied about him as he paddles the boat round and round, this way and that way, after the duck.

Both Dick and Bill are what I would call 'good' men; that is to say men of basic goodwill who run their lives, so far as I know, according to Christian principles. As against this – or perhaps I should say, at the same time as this – they both come from the English Warrior Class. They probably believe in a 'Lord Mighty in Battle' and a 'Lord God of Hosts' who would certainly take their side against the Wog, the Bosch, the Dago, the Yellow Peril, the Nigger-in-the-woodpile or whatever 'Jack, joke, poor potsherd' happens to be an enemy of our tight little island at the time. Their upbringing therefore predisposes them towards a certain way of behaviour which objective humanists might under certain circumstances describe as harsh or even brutal if they didn't know, as I do, that they really *are* good men. All this is not entirely by the way.

The day could not be more perfect for shooting: a wind off the sea, high cloud (no sun to blind one), and now, though it is scarcely daylight, excellent visibility. And still the birds in their thousands keep flighting over the causeway, and still we are firing just about as fast as we can load. Even my score is now up to eleven and the others most certainly have bagged many more. But because of the direction of the wind a lot of birds are beginning to drop in the sedge between the lake and the harder ground, and Borley is not having much success in forcing the boat through the reeds.

'Never mind the boat, Borley,' shouts Bill. 'Get in after it.'

Borley does as he is told and splashes in waist deep after the bird Bill has just shot. For a moment I catch a glimpse of Borley looking, with compassion it seems, at the beautiful feathers of the dead sheldrake. The next moment some teal come my way and all my atavistic impulses are concentrated on trying to knock at least one of them out of the sky. A shout comes from Dick on my right.

'That bird's only winged, Borley. Get after it before it gets in the reeds.'

And then Bill again: 'Quick, man, you'll have to swim for it.'

My attention is diverted to a couple of rather high pintails which I miss. I am conscious of my relatively small bag and when I see a teal I had shot blowing into the middle of the lake I find myself shouting at Borley with the rest: 'Borley, that bird – quick, before it drifts away.'

After that it becomes pandemonium with everybody shouting at Borley at once.

'Borley, did you see that one drop?'

'Get after it, Borley.'

'That pintail, Borley, did you mark it?'

'Swim, man, swim.'

The next, and most unforgettable, memory I have of Borley is seeing him swimming, and because he needs both hands to swim, he holds the dead bird in his mouth like the retriever he has become.

The flight ends as suddenly as it began with the last skein of duck flying seawards. It is probably just as well anyway because we are nearly out of cartridges. Also, now in full visibility, we realize the German observation-posts in the hills might interpret our relatively innocent activities as being something more warlike.

With the help of Borley we collect the bag together and lay it out on the causeway. All told there are fifty-three birds and Bill and Dick are congratulating each other heartily. Even I come in for a qualified good word.

On the way home we pass a water-meadow, only slightly flooded, on the enemy side of the causeway.

'I bet that holds snipe,' Dick says. 'I think I'll just walk it up.'

Bill casts a professional glance at the enigmatic hills and then rather doubtfully says, 'If you're going to, we all might as well.'

We string out and in practically no time some snipe get up, piping excitedly, and jink off down-wind. Dick not only has the best gun, but also the luck as well. Within about a hundred yards or so he gets a beautiful right-and-left. The first bird drops just ahead of him but the one shot with the choke barrel falls some way off to the left.

'Get after that one, Borley,' he shouts.

Borley stands quite still for a moment, shivering in his wet clothes. He has a puzzled look on his face. Then after a second or two he splashes off obediently. Dick stops at the first snipe and stuffs the small wet bird in his pocket. He then turns and looks towards the second one. Borley has almost reached it when he too stops and turns. Dick calls out, 'What's the matter, Borley? Didn't you mark it?'

'Yes, sir, but – '

'What?'

I have seen Borley with his lip trembling before, but now his whole face seems to break up as if he is going to cry.

'But what, Borley?' says Dick.

'Sir,' he says shivering and trembling, 'I'm not a dog, sir, you didn't ought to treat me like a dog.'

No one who has once been shot at by a German eighty-eight millimetre gun can mistake it a second time. It is a dual-purpose high-velocity weapon and when fired over open sights it has the most violent and, in every way, demolishing effect. It is, as General Briggs once said, the best dual-purpose weapon after the human male pudendum.

Well, at this precise moment we hear its unmistakably fearful crack followed instantaneously by its vicious shell-burst. At once we are all lying face downwards as the shrapnel splashes round us in the inch-deep water – all except Dick, that is – who in his calm way goes on walking towards his bird. Seeing him thus walking with the same regular, even rather slow, pace, the rest of us get rather shamefacedly to our feet. At least Bill and I do. Borley just goes on lying here. When finally the three of us converge on him we see that his right hand lies almost within grasp of the dead snipe. It is also pretty obvious that he too is dead.

Dick bends down and I think he is going to get his identity-disc, but he doesn't. He picks up the snipe instead. I take the appropriate half of his identity-tag plus his pay-book, which is the proper thing for the Company second-in-command to do.

When I am concerned about human values – in other words, when I am emotionally upset – my mind loses its logic and tends to grasp at trivialities. Now, thinking of my administrative duties as second-in-command, I ask a stupid question.

'What sort of a return do you think we ought to put in about Borley?' I say.

'Killed in action. What else, fool?' says Dick.

I look away to seaward in order to hide the various emotions of shame, of guilt, of total inadequacy that I know must be showing on my face. In the distance a few shafts of sunlight have broken through the cloud and now their rays slant downward on the grey sea. Against them the last skeins of duck are flying westward. They too are leaving their dead behind.

7

The Sergeant-Major's prognostications had been correct. Christmas Day saw the 1st Battalion in the troopship *Cameronia* heading into the grey Atlantic. Day by day the sea got greyer and greyer until, on January 5, 1944, in the very early hours of a day that never actually dawned, the ship put into blacked-out war-time Glasgow. It was raining wet soot.

> *We'll meet again,*
> *Don't know where,*
> *Don't know when,*
> *But I know we'll meet again*
> *Some sunny day.*

By tacit consent Phoebe and I did not meet again. Our love affair effectively ended in Paris in 1939 but we did not have enough sense to realize it. Our marriage which, since I was a minor at the time, required a long-distance sanction from my father in Fiji, was a disastrous mistake.

The rest of that bleakest of bleak winters was spent in a Nissen-hutted camp in the dripping pinewoods of Norfolk. When spring came at last almost everybody in the Battalion was quite prepared to go campaigning again, not only to get away from Norfolk, but also to withdraw from their domestic imbroglios. For soldiers to return home in the middle of a war is a mistake. Lives already complicated before men went abroad the first time were doubly complicated by the time they left for the Second Front.

> *Keep smiling through*
> *Just like you always do*
> *Till the blue skies*
> *Chase those dark clouds far away.*

If anybody ever asks me in a quarter of a century's time what were the most miserable times of my life, I will say without hesitation that they were five years spent in the rhododendrons of

Sunningdale School, Berkshire, and five months spent in the pinewoods of Brandon Camp, Norfolk.

> *Oh I will just say hello*
> *To the folks that you know,*
> *Tell them you won't be long.*
> *They will be happy to know*
> *That as I saw you go*
> *You were singing this song.*

Having no home to go to, when my turn came for leave I headed for London and the flat of my friends Pat and Noel Carlile.[1] 'Come any time you like,' they said. 'There is always a bed in the Black Hole.' Well, no hole could be blacker than Brandon Camp and whatever the merits of the Carlile boxroom I looked forward to seeing its owners again. In due course, therefore, I find myself ringing the door bell at 12 Malvern Court, London, SW3. There is no answer. I ring again more vehemently and after a little while I hear a scratching around inside. Then the door is tentatively opened by the first all-white woman I have seen for two years.

So I take possession of the Black Hole and after a perfunctory courtship, I take possession of Mrs Crawshaw (the lady mentioned above) as well. She turns out to be the Carlile's PG and her name is Lettice. They never told me they had a PG, but I suppose that is beside the point.

> *I haven't said thanks*
> *For that lovely weekend,*
> *Those two days of heaven*
> *You helped me to spend,*
> *The ride in the taxi when midnight had flown*
> *And breakfast next morning just we two alone.*

Well, one wartime leave is much like another, groping about in dark nightclubs and then groping about in the darker dark outside in the hope of finding a taxi to take one where? Home? Then the next morning a disconsolate crawl round the pubs in the hope of finding some gin with which to cure one's hangover.

[1] Former racing correspondent of *The Times*.

We'll meet again,
Don't know where,
Don't know when,
But I know we'll meet again
Some sunny day.

At dawn on June 4 we are all on deck watching lots of empty landing-craft returning from France having delivered the 'first wave'. The sailors look dishevelled and tough and give our lads a bit of lip about 'wanting to get up there'. The Riflemen reply that they've been getting up there ever since the Battle of Sidi Rezegh.

There'll be Blue Birds over
The white cliffs of Dover
Tomorrow, just you wait and see.

We drop anchor and transfer to landing-craft for the trip ashore. I am wearing my second-best tunic (service dress) and my old desert cap – for luck. I am also carrying, hopefully, a suitcase. The Navy tell us they are putting us down in no more than two foot of water. Unfortunately, stepping off quite properly at the head of my men, I go straight into a submarine shell-hole up to the arm-pits. Well, it gets a laugh and, after all, it *is* Arromanches-les-Bains.

There'll be love and laughter
And peace ever after
Tomorrow, when the world is free.

As soon as we are off the beach I form the men up in column-of-threes and we swing smartly off along the Bayeux road at a riflemanlike quick-march of 120 paces to the minute. The rear of the column is brought up by Rifleman Godfrey wheeling his pack and my suitcase in a commandeered baker's push-cart. Finally we come to our rendezvous (a mere map reference) and march in very regimentally.

'Battalion, halt . . . Right turn. . . .'

I salute the Colonel as it is the first time I have seen him today.

'Marching party present, Colonel.'

'What's that man doing wheeling a barrow?'

'That's my suitcase, Colonel.'

'I see . . . Very well. You may dismiss.'

> *There'll be Blue Birds over*
> *The white cliffs of Dover*
> *Tomorrow, when the world is free.*

We got our first bloody nose at a place called Villers Bocage when, as spearhead of the British break-out, we were caught in a sharp pincer movement between two of Hitler's remaining Panzer divisions. To avoid annihilation they had to pull us out by night under cover of a heavy bomber raid. But before we had had time to do much more than apply the iodine pencil and sticking plaster, we were switched to the stricken fields of Caen where we lay for days on end in full view of the enemy and, of course, under shell-fire.

> *Love walked right in*
> *And chased the shadows away,*
> *Love walked right in*
> *And made my happiest day.*

Many died during this time including Gilbert Talbot and Francis Dorrien-Smith. On the morning of the third day Bill Apsey was badly hit and I was sent to take over his Company. I was just twenty-four years old. When I got there I couldn't find them. The vehicles were there dispersed about the bleak and barren stubble fields, but not a sinner attended them. Eventually I found the whole of Company Headquarters skulking in a spinney half a mile away. Even the Sergeant-Major was there. It was quite obvious that the whole lot were completely bomb-happy and my heart sank without trace.

> *One perfect moment*
> *My heart felt aglow*
> *When love said 'hello'*
> *And not a word was spoken.*

Things went, as they always do, from bad to worse. The Sergeant-Major, a man whom I had always respected for his soldierly qualities, had completely lost his nerve. Without actually running away he had now become to all purposes non-existent. The same happened to another desert hero, 'Shag' Davies the signaller, who couldn't be persuaded to get up out of the ground.

> *One kiss and I forgot the gloom of the past,*
> *One kiss and I had found my future at last.*

On the fourth day I had to put a big-mouthed platoon-sergeant under arrest for absenting himself from the field of battle. On the morning of the fifth day I found a young soldier sitting in his slit-trench blubbing like the child he was. That same afternoon a new subaltern[1] who had joined us in Norfolk was sitting in his half-track[2] next to Sergeant Batt. Then, according to Batt, after they had sweated out a particularly heavy stonk from enemy medium artillery, he took out his revolver and shot himself through the foot.

> *One kiss and I have found my life completely new,*
> *When love walked in with you.*

Weeks later, but still in France, I was walking down a road past a herd of Friesians, every one of which had just been hit by mortar fire. They were lying down mooing in the special way cattle have when wounded. Suddenly there was a loud bang on the other side of the road a short distance further on. It didn't sound to me like a mortar bomb and I went to investigate. Obviously it must have been the farmer going to inspect his cows. He had stepped on a mine and there was now nothing left of him except his naked trunk – no head, no limbs, but heart still intact for the diaphragm was working violently, the ribs going in and out like bellows.

> *That perfect night,*
> *The night we met,*
> *There was magic abroad in the air,*
> *And when you turned and smiled at me*
> *A nightingale sang in Berkeley Square.*

[1] This same officer later became a notorious smuggler, operating out of Tangier in a speed-boat.

[2] A lightly armoured troop-carrier with wheels in front and tracks behind.

All is well – at least for the time being. We are in Holland now, just on the Dutch side of the German border. Although the temperature drops to twenty-six degrees of frost at night, we are snug enough here by day in the schoolroom of a convent. This place is called Holtum and in front, between us and the Germans, is a dyke called Vloed Beek which gives some definition to our *status quo*. Creature comforts include a pig recently killed by Rifleman O'Donnell, a demijohn of issue rum (known as 'gun-fire') produced by the Colour-Sergeant, and a big bottle of Angostura bitters posted by my father all the way from, believe it or not, Angostura. It is nearly Christmas and there are rumours of other good things in store.

> *The streets of Town were paved in gold,*
> *It was such a romantic affair –*
> *There were angels dining at the Ritz*
> *And a nightingale sang in Berkeley Square.*

This morning company commanders were summoned for orders. Battalion Headquarters is about half a mile back on the Juliana Canal. When I got there Victor Paley, the Colonel, was on the ice, skating, with beads of moisture dripping from the straggly ends of his pale moustache. His hands were clasped behind his back like an eminent Victorian.

'Get your skates on,' he said to me, and Alan Parker, grinning fatly, handed me his. I then slithered about on the ice while Victor gave out orders, attempting at the same time to do a figure of eight backwards.

'Brigade wants a prisoner for identification.'

'Oh!'

'In fact they insist.'

'I see.'

'Well?'

'Nothing in particular, Colonel.'

'What?'

'Just that it's Christmas Eve, that's all.'

'What's that got to do with it?'

The moon that lingered over London Town,
Poor puzzled moon, she wore a frown,
How could she know we two were so in love
The whole darn world seemed upside down.

Christmas Eve and a quiet afternoon with no wind. Horizontal rays of the setting sun filter through the sandbagged casements of the schoolroom. On the far wall the cold sunbeams faintly light a coloured print of Our Lady holding, behind broken glass, the Sacred Heart of Jesus in immaculate fingers. Beneath her Wicks, the signaller, slumped, balaclavaed, hands deep in greatcoat pockets, is attached by his earphones to the wireless set that stands before him on the desk. The set hums away in an even tone, hypnotizing Wicks into a torpor from which he emerges only to blow occasionally on the cigarette-butt stuck in his mouth.

At the other end of the room at another desk sits Alfred, the Gunner officer, making chinographic squeaks on the talc of his map. Beside him sits his bombardier writing a letter, eyes close to the paper, tongue following the convolutions of his pen. Otherwise there is silence.

As the rays flatten and fade the Sacred Heart passes into monochrome and the red ignition light of the wireless set becomes in its place the focal point of all eyes.

In this quietness a distant gun sounds off like a door slamming in the far wing of an old house. An interval follows while we listen. Then the whine of a shell, barely audible at first, makes itself heard on its leisurely way. Finally another moment of silence, then a single remote explosion, and once more silence.

'Nieustadt!' says Alfred looking up.

I nod.

*   *   *

Yesterday C Company, who are holding Nieustadt on our right, had a little tragedy. A shell, which failed to explode on impact, entered the cellar that served as company headquarters. The projectile rattled round the tiny room, took the leg clean off Corporal Worboys, the signaller, and killed the new Company Commander outright. The shell, having come to rest, then opened and distributed over the whole bloody mess a gentle shower of propaganda leaflets. Worboys had been with the Battalion all through the desert. The Company Commander on the other hand had only taken over the day before. He was just out from England and this was his first sniff of powder, and his last.

The leaflet depicted a skeleton in British tin hat groping a naked girl from behind. The caption read, 'Tommy, your next leave?'

Alfred and the bombardier are now intoning to each other, *decani et cantorum*, the Gunner liturgy in phonetic alphabet. This the bombardier records in shorthand for the benefit of his battery headquarters.

'Writing a note to Santa Claus, are you?' says the supine Wicks when they finish.

'Christmas card for old Jerry,' replies the bombardier closing his notebook with the finality of a priest removing the stole. Wicks pauses to unplug, inspect, and put back in his flat dog's mouth the blackened stump of his fag.

'Proper sod, in't it, eh?' he offers by way of repartee.

'Yer, I'll say,' ripostes the other.

'Tucked up in bed with the old woman, that'd do me.'

'Yer, would an' all.'

Daylight has now quite gone and I call for Godfrey to bring lamps and mugs. I ask Alfred if he has ever tasted rum and Angostura. No, but he assures me he would be delighted to try.

'The bitters,' I explain encouragingly, 'help to cut the sweetness of issue rum.'

Yes, he agrees that they should make an admirable improvement.

I ask Godfrey what there is for supper.

'Bully fritters, bully rissoles, nice cold bully and cheese. Or how about biscuit burgoo?'

At this calculated insult I lose my temper.

'Dammit, Godfrey, what's happened to all the pork?'

'Finished, sir.'

'Finished? You finished it, you mean.'

'Excuse me, sir. It was the officers finished it. The night Captain Parker and Mr Clive came to supper – I mean dinner.'

'Well then, why can't we have an omelette or something?'

'No eggs, sir,' answers Godfrey, contentedly presenting the great British negative.

'Hell and damnation, why aren't there any eggs? Everybody else has got eggs. You're just idle, Godfrey. That's your trouble.'

'There was only one man 'oo was perfect and look what they done to 'im.'

'What?' I ask absent-mindedly, brooding on my grievance.

'Crucified 'im.'

'You'll find yourself going back to duty, Godfrey, if I have any more lip from you.'

But already Godfrey, delighted with himself, is half-way out of the room, rehearsing the episode under his breath for the benefit of his friends.

Later, after more rum and a plate of bully and chips, Alfred confesses that he knows where there are some eggs. 'I've seen them from my OP,'[1] he says. 'Unfortunately they're only about three hundred yards from the enemy.'

'Where?' I ask, and he describes very accurately a deserted farmhouse in no-man's-land near the Vloed Beek.

We bed down for the night on the schoolroom floor. The signallers change watch but the wireless hums on as before, its red light keeping up its staring match with the eyes of the Blessed Virgin.

Many solo sailors say that they wake at the slightest change of course. Three years of campaigning have made me equally alert. When the wireless hum suddenly changed pitch I was out of bed in a flash. The signaller was already writing down a message.

'It's 14 Platoon, sir. Platoon Commander says there's a "terrific racket" going on on their front.'

By his derisive emphasis on 'terrific racket' he succeeds in indicating that the vocabulary is Gerald Lascelles's, not his own.

'All right, I'll speak. Wake the Gunner officer.'

By the time I have finished talking to Gerald on the set Alfred is by my side.

'What's the trouble?' he asks.

'It's the Centre Platoon – Gerald Lascelles. He says there's an

[1] Observation Post.

108

awful din going on out front, singing and shouting and playing a tuba. They're standing-to.'

'How does he know it's a tuba?'

'His family is musical.'

'What do you want me to do?'

'Give them what for. Strop them up.' The Nieustadt business still rankled.

'Got a bearing?'

'Yes.'

'Will five rounds gunfire do?'

'Yes.'

Five minutes later we are both standing in the darkness outside the schoolroom staring at the frosty night sky.

'Any minute now,' says Alfred, peering at the luminous dial of his watch.

A moment later the sky to the east erupts with four vivid flashes, followed instantaneously by the crash of four guns. As the first shells scream low overhead towards the enemy, the four twenty-five pounders sound in unison again; and then again three more times. At the end, in the stillness that follows, we hear one last round, late-fired, burst alone on the target area.

Christmas morning sparkles. Brilliant sun shines upon the Breughel landscape and every particle of rime refracts a dazzling point of light. Black rooks pick holes in the thin snow at the same time as Rifleman Godfrey urinates a yellow 'Happy Christmas', spelling it with only one P. There are no eggs again for breakfast.

After a light-hearted row with Godfrey, I take myself for a walk to visit 14 Platoon. My nailed boots creak pleasantly on the impacted snow and the frozen air hurts my lungs and nostrils. An oblique line of silver birches glinting in the sun give a perspective to the flat countryside, and I feel happy and well.

At 14 Platoon there's a good deal of hilarity and badinage over the events of the night. In the excitement of the tuba solo Rifleman Rudkin caught his trousers on some barbed wire and now dances around in his long underpants (draws, woollen, long) to give emphasis to his request for a new pair. There's a bottle of liquor going the rounds and some rifleman, handing it round, addresses me by my Christian name. I question Gerald closely about last night's incident and now in retrospect he concludes that it was not hostile. But in the dark of the night, understandably, he interpreted it otherwise. He remains adamant, however, that the musical instrument was a tuba.

Back at Headquarters a small crowd has collected and, in the centre of it, Oscar Howell-Beavis. Europe suits Oscar since he can read signposts and ask the way. In fact it turns out that he has just found his way all the way to Rheims and back, as proof of which he has brought me a case of champagne with the compliments of the season.

Good. So there is nothing for it but to celebrate. A bayonet soon opens the case. The wine, De Venoge 1937, snug in its straw jackets, is at the perfect temperature. I open the first bottle skilfully with a soft sigh.

'It's vulgar to pop it,' says Alfred, who is a Wykehamist, approvingly.

Sunshine, snow and champagne are an intoxicating synthesis and it is not long before we are down to the second layer of the case. I'm just easing the cork out of bottle number 7 when I see the shambling figure of Godfrey coming towards us. What is more, I can tell by the look on his face that, owing to congenital inertia and lack of initiative, he has failed to get hold of any eggs. Not trusting myself to speak to him civilly, therefore, I ignore him. Then suddenly an idea of some felicity occurs to me.

'Why don't we go to that Vloed Beek farm and get our own eggs?' I say.

'Vloed Beek? No thanks, old fruit.' That was Oscar.

'Yes, why not?' says Alfred, who I have known for some time to be a hero as well as a Wykehamist. We pass then a resolution to drink champagne out of tin mugs for the rest of our lives and, as we drink to this resolve, we hear coming from the next room the melancholy sound of a mouth-organ and Godfrey singing *con molto sentimento*

> 'Oi down't want ter pliy in your yard,
> Oi down't loike yew any more.'

Being of a lachrymose disposition, this brings tears to my eyes which at that moment are following the direction of a sunbeam spotlighting the gaudy print of Our Lady. She smiles her encouragement.

'Let's go,' says Alfred, 'if we're going.'

At 14 Platoon we discuss the ground with Gerald Lascelles over bottle number 8. Somehow, incredibly yet typically, he produces champagne glasses.

'There is a covered approach most of the way,' he says. 'The last bit is open but with luck may be in dead ground.'

We leave to a chorus of conflicting advice from Gerald's myrmidons, much of it obscene. They are, I note with some misgiving, well on with their local brand of rot-gut.

'We'll give you covering fire if you get into trouble, won't we, Rudkin?' says Gerald.

Out beyond the minefield the glittering snow is unmarked save for the patterned footprints of birds.

I look back but there is no sign of anybody now. We follow a line of silver birches growing along a bank. Small cascades of snow falling from the branches sound startlingly loud. All at once a brace of partridges get up with an appalling clatter. Alfred and I throw ourselves flat on the ground and look at each other. His look says, 'That gave me a nasty fright.' Mine says, 'I am in favour of blood sports.'

I whisper, 'We must be about half-way.'

Soon we come to the last bit of cover. Ahead is a stretch of dead ground ending in a slight rise. I make a sign to Alfred and we crawl the fifty yards or so to the crest. Once there we lie for a moment, breath fanning out in cones from our nostrils. I pull the peak of my cap down over my eyes and raise my head slowly.

There about one hundred yards away, completely in the open, is the farm, a square red-brick building with a clutter of sheds and outhouses on the near side. Round these a few hens are pecking amongst the straw and midden. About another hundred yards beyond the farm is a line of willows indicating the course of the Vloed Beek, and beyond that. . . .

I was thinking of snipers now. I was also wondering if Gerald's platoon were sober enough to cover us properly. There was also another possibility that stupidly I had not allowed for: some drunk in C Company might mistake us for Germans and give us

the works. I feel a prod from Alfred and (like the trained infantryman that I am) lower my head very slowly. In his outstretched
hand is an elegant flask containing good French brandy. I knew
all along that Alfred is not only a Wykehamist and a hero, but
an epicure too. Then my mind starts running into clichés about
Dutch courage and I remember we are in Holland.

'I'm going to run to the nearest corner of the shed,' I say.
'Do you know how this carbine works?'

Alfred nods.

'Then cover me. When I give the signal, come too.'

Alfred nods again.

Then I become enormously aware of myself running across
that piece of open ground. Is the sniper's finger even now tightening on the trigger? Will my next footfall be on a mine? What
is the record for doing the hundred yards?

Suddenly I am leaning against the wall of the shed with my
lungs in my mouth and my heart banging in my ears. It takes me
a few seconds to get my breath. Then I wave Alfred on. He comes
loping across and I can just imagine him on the football field at
Winchester, probably rather bad at games.

Inside the shed among the scattered straw and dirt are half a
dozen untidy nests piled high with eggs, the accumulation of
weeks of laying.

'If we take the ones on top they'll be fresh,' I say.

'Surely the cold would preserve them,' says Alfred.

'But how can we carry them all?'

While debating this point I notice a well-grown pullet, one
raised leg poised, watching me sidewise out of a yellow eye.

'That bird looks in need of a good home,' observes Alfred.

The bird, recovering from its first surprise, jerks inquisitively,
neck upstretched. Then, suddenly apprehensive, it makes off
with long rangy strides round a corner of the yard. I hand Alfred
back the carbine and follow.

Then in a flash all acquisitive thoughts leave me. There dese-
crating the clean snow, and extending for some distance towards
the enemy, is a pattern of new shell-bursts, vicious, black, and
ugly. And there in the middle of them, caught in all the abandonment of unexpected death, sprawls a young German soldier with

short cropped ginger hair. Using full voice for the first time since entering no-man's-land I call to Alfred. Then I cross over quickly and remove from the body all badges and means of identification. I no longer think of a sniper, but Alfred who has caught up has noticed something else. He moves a few yards further on to where this something is glinting in the snow, and I see him bend and pick it up. It is a large brass instrument which, as he brushes off the snow, reveals in its shiny horn a jagged shrapnel hole. Even to the uninitiated it is obviously a tuba.

Alfred comes back to where I am kneeling. There are blood drops in the snow. On, presumably, drunken impulse he lays the tuba with Wykehamistic punctilio on the dead man's chest. I realize that I am now perfectly sober.

At first light the next morning, St Stephen's Day, the Germans put in an attack in battalion strength and wiped out C Company at Nieustadt. This rather neutralizes my previous day's dubious triumph in having obtained the required identification almost single-handed.

> I may be right
> And I may be wrong,
> But I'm perfectly willing to swear
> That when you turned and smiled at me
> A nightingale sang in Berkeley Square.

PART TWO

8

'Argolici rediere duces altaria fumant. . . .'

The war is over, but it will never be over for me as long as I live. It will influence the way I walk, the clothes I wear, the way I talk, the way I cut my hair. It will influence the way I eat, the way I sleep, the way I get out of bed in the morning, and it will influence all these things for ever. It will qualify the way I run my life, the way I run other people's lives – if I ever do again; it will have bearing upon all my dealings with all my fellow men now and for ever. It will affect the way I look at a landscape, the way I build a house, the way I treat my wife, the way I bring up my children. It will affect above all the way I think and it will affect my thoughts for ever. It will be in the way I live and will be with me when I die.

Not that I am thinking about dying. I'm very pleased to be alive and I shall be grateful for this, too, for ever. On D-Day I wrote myself off because I did not think my luck could last. Every day that I live from now on, therefore, is a bonus and shall be observed as a fiesta.

I was nineteen when I joined up and I am twenty-six now. Most nights I dream that I'm being shelled. If it is not too bad I think I only twitch a bit, but if the shells are landing heavy and close I wake myself up leaping for cover. I would not describe them as nightmares, just part of daily – or rather, nightly – life. They say that a man who has lost a limb often feels a pain in the amputated part although it has long since been consigned to the incinerator. I am being shelled in the amputated part of my life.

Who am I? Where am I in relation to who or what I thought I might have been? I don't know. I only know for certain that I'm not dead. That to me is very important and I am grateful. Grateful to whom? To God, perhaps? Indeed the fact that I am alive is the only thing of any importance at all and the only thing I can grasp because, as I say, I do not know the answers to the other questions. Nor am I sure about God. I only know that I feel grateful to someone, so why not to Him? Is that not the beginning of belief?

I am what used to be called an ex-serviceman. I was born in 1919 and well remember as a child men coming round in their old khaki tunics and medal ribbons for a tanner, or a bob if they were lucky. Some of them would give a salute if they thought that would extract a larger sum. Clearly I'm not one of those. But still less am I that corduroyed young student at the Byam Shaw, or that romantic would-be painter of the *Quartier Latin*, or the lover of Phoebe of the golden days. There are no signs left of him at all.

If I think back four or five years I can see myself in the Mess at Tidworth. It is a guest night and I see it in Edwardian or, in painters' terms, 'Euston Road', style: sombre colours, light passing with scumbled edges like a Sickert; rifle-green uniforms, ruby-coloured port, mahogany table, and the lamplight catching silver tobacco-smoke and the silver instruments of the band. Mr West, the Bandmaster, has just been in to take a glass of wine with the Colonel and most of us have drifted out into the high dark hall – smoke drifting upwards high-lighting our pink-topped, cigar-tipped, dark green perpendiculars, to hear the band wind up with the Regimental March; then a few whoops and hollers as they give us by way of a coda the Double-March Past.

But there are no signs of me there now either.

Where am I then in relation to my past life? Obviously no-where. Where am I in regard to the future? Equally nowhere so far as I can see. Where I am very precisely and at this moment of time is in a small flat in Oakley Street with Lettice, who is pregnant. It is bitterly cold, food is rationed more rigorously than during the war, there is very little electricity and practically nothing at all to drink, even if one could afford it.

So here is your latter-day Icarus, with wings not melted, but frozen off. Here am I, youth gone, and gone all the joy that goes with it, trapped in what was once a gay, even noble, city; now the greyest, darkest, drabbest most depressing place in the world. Who was it said 'Stop laughing – this is England!'? The whole mingy little island could have been sunk without trace for all that I now care. I would only feel sorry for the poor Jews and Poles and other refugees to whom it has become, *faute de mieux*, an asylum. But as far as I am concerned England as it is today is certainly not worth fighting for. If anybody had asked me five years ago why I was fighting in the war I could not have given an answer because I am certain that I did not know. Perhaps 'the spirit of adventure' would have been as near to the truth as anything.

I now see, or begin to see, perhaps, that we all – by 'all' I mean contestants on both sides – were caught up in an involuntary act in which we were all equally victims. At the same time I do not necessarily regard the soldiers, sailors and airmen – whether they now be dead or alive – as victims. The real victims are the Jews and Poles and other destroyed, mutilated, homeless peoples of the world, together with those who deliberately destroyed and mutilated them and made them homeless. They conjointly are the ones to be pitied because they had everything to lose and lost everything.

As for the sailors, soldiers and airmen, they do not represent man's inhumanity to man, but quite the reverse because we were all comrades-in-arms and never for a moment felt hatred or animosity for the man at the other end of the rifle. I feel deeply deprived by the deaths of Francis and Gilbert, as well as those of Mulford and Bradbury and others too numerous to name, but I do not resent their deaths particularly; only the circumstances that caused them. I feel almost as sorry about all the innocent young Italians and Germans that Mulford, Bradbury, Francis, Gilbert and I were responsible for killing, and we killed a good many.

Who then are to be blamed and who are to be pitied? Obviously those most culpable should be pitied most, but somewhere along the line are a few lesser mortals who should be allowed a moment of compassion: for example, the Liverpool dockers who were supposed to be loading our ship to go to the war. Instead they sat about on deck playing cards and striking for higher wages. It was the soldiers who loaded the ship and they did it for about half what the dockers were being paid and with more than a good chance of being shot into the bargain. Those dockers are a case for compassion . . . for they knew not what they did not do.

I am now a trainee sub-editor at Reuters. I suppose I am lucky to get the job, but it seems a far cry from being a Major (acting Lieut-Colonel) in the Rifle Brigade. My fellow-subs on the News Desk regard me as something the cat brought in: a military man; some sort of semi-gent. What's he here for? All the same I am quite prepared to start at the bottom.

'Why start at the top?' asks one of my companions not too unkindly, but I suppose in real amazement. I understand that he has reached Fleet Street through a variety of provincial newspapers where it is regarded as promotion when you cease to take the names of people at funerals, and take instead the names of those at weddings. After all, the bridegroom is sometimes euphoric enough to dish out a free drink.

Another sub has somehow got hold of my particulars. 'MC?[1] What does that stand for?' he asks mockingly, 'Master of Ceremonies?'

My first and greatest disadvantage – indeed disgrace – is that I cannot type. All the other fellows type at great speed with two or more fingers. The second disadvantage is that Mr Pigge, the Day Editor, does not like me and in consequence makes no attempt to teach me the tricks of the trade. I suppose there is a faint odour of 'officer and gentleman' about me that he doesn't care for.

A sub-editor's job on the News Desk is to translate incoming reports from cablese into journalism. Thus it is important that words like 'paratroops' should be translated as 'Red Devils' or 'skymen'. Otherwise Reuter's hot piece of news may fail to make a sale.

'Always remember, Luke, that news is a commodity,' repeats the Managing Editor, whom I seem to meet every day in the urinal. I am sure he is right, and I am sure I will get the knack soon if only Mr Pigge will give me half a chance. My typing is coming on already.

In general, though, I prefer being on the night shift. In the first place the Night Editor is much more helpful, and secondly

[1] Military Cross.

there is a certain magic about the all-night activity of Fleet Street. There is also a late-closing pub to go to in the break and, finally, the all-night number 11 bus that takes me home to Oakley Street as dawn is breaking, where I find Lettice cold and pregnant in bed.

*   *   *

What sort of folly is this? What am I doing being married and having children? What do I want children for? What do I want to be married for, come to that? How marvellous if I could only disappear – take a boat somewhere, to South America, perhaps. I could change my name and start all over again. Why not? Why not buy a dead body, put my identification on it, and let it be washed ashore somewhere. It has been done before. There's a whole beautiful life going on somewhere away from this grey London, a life that I've hardly tasted yet. I could offer myself as a mercenary or military adviser to some Latin-American Republic. After all, I've got a good war record and I'm young. I might eventually become a General and have my portrait engraved on the stamps. The Wild Geese were always doing that sort of thing and Spanish America is full of monuments to O'Higginses and O'Donnells. *Calle Pedro Luke? Plaza Generalissimo Luke?* Why not?

'It's no go, Luke,' the Managing Editor says. 'I'm sorry.' This is in the middle of the morning shift.

'When do you want me to go? End of the month?'

'You might as well go now. Collect your money from the office on the way out.' He was quite amiable about it.

Now how do I go back to the News Desk and get my coat without looking as if I've just been sacked? What a bloody awful predicament! It is that Pigge of course.

Outside in the street the full horror of the situation becomes more and more apparent. Out of work, the baby just about due and all I've got is this week's pay-packet. One thing is obvious, I cannot go back to Oakley Street at this time of day or Lettice will know something is wrong. I can't go into any of the local pubs either for fear of meeting people from Reuters. There is only one thing for it – St Paul's Cathedral. They say it takes half a day to get round and it is only just up the road.

*   *   *

The winter of my unemployment was one of the coldest in living memory. Snow fell and, having been trodden hard, froze and there remained getting greyer and greyer as the months went by. In February Lettice gave birth to our son, Harry, whose pram had to be negotiated up the ice-clogged steps of 97 Oakley Street, and then up a further flight of stairs. The electric heater glowed a dim pink if you put it in a dark corner.

'*Argolici rediere duces . . . ?*' If the ancient Greeks had been as pinch-penny as our government there would have been no altars burning when their leaders returned from the war because of fuel cuts. Did I say, then, that every day would be celebrated as a fiesta? God forgive me, but I meant it at the time.

*   *   *

During the day Luke went round the employment agencies and the various associations for demobilized soldiers. He also called on such friends as might be able to introduce him into some form of work. In the evenings he doctored the Algerian wine by mixing it with sugar or lees of port before drinking it.

Eventually there occurred at the Victoria and Albert Museum an exhibition called 'Britain Can Make It' which was an attempt to show the markets of the world that the war had not deprived Britannia of her energies and skills. The proof of this particular pudding was that most people left it on the side of the plate. Nevertheless, being tipped off about this by an unemployed officers' agency, Luke went round and landed a job as a guide.

The Britain Can Make It Exhibition was of course a haven for unemployed and unemployable ex-officers, resting actors, and such members of the homosexual world who for their own reasons preferred casual employment.

Luke briefly reports his period at the Victoria and Albert Museum.

*   *   *

I might have known. The first person I run into is Oscar Howell-Beavis. He has already been 'working' here a week and knows everybody. It is money for old rope, he says with his aptitude for cliché. One only has to be seen around in a decent suit for a bit, looking amiable and willing, and then one can slip out to the pub round by Brompton Oratory.

I ask Oscar about his Isotto-Francini, or whatever it was. He says that it all arrived in time for VE-Day except that his mother had lost some vital part when they had to move house to make way for a tank gunnery range. Of course any ploy of Oscar's is doomed to at least partial failure, if not actual disaster, and I find it rather unnerving that he is here – not that there is any future in this job.

The most impressive thing about the Britain Can Make It Exhibition is the music which is diffused throughout the building. It is obviously the arbitrary choice of someone little concerned with the objectives of the Exhibition because, apart from an occasional touch of Elgar, not much of it is of British make. In particular there is one haunting piece which I have never heard before. It is by a Spaniard, Manuel de Falla. I would like to get to Spain sometime, but how?

Oscar and I and a fair-haired ex-fighter pilot spend a lot of time in the pub drinking 'dog's noses' (a gin in half a pint of bitter) while Pilot Officer Prune describes his war experiences. I must say they are quite interesting to an ex-infantryman. For example, the cure for a hangover in his particular unit was to climb inside a Spitfire, if it was not in use, and take several deep breaths from the oxygen-mask. Infallible, apparently.

I think if it were not for Oscar and P.O. Prune I would find the humiliation of this job insupportable. The actors are accustomed to this way of keeping going and, besides, they have an honourable profession back of them. As for the gay society, they have their own network and their own way of life. I have none of these things.

The other day I was just standing around in my blue de-mob suit, with my badge of servitude in my lapel, when I suddenly saw a former friend from the Regiment, a member of a famous banking family, coming round the corner. I made a dive for the Gents and with luck I don't think he saw me. But the experience has unnerved me and from now on I shall have one eye cocked against exposure.

So every evening it is back to Oakley Street, probably rather the better for a few 'dog's noses'. Little Harry is rather sweet, I must say, clean-looking and not much trouble. But under the circumstances what the hell good am I to him, or he to me for that matter? Poor little perisher.

'Nights in the Gardens of Spain'. That is the most evocative music I have ever heard. Yet, how can it be since I have never been to Spain? Spain . . . if only I could get there!

9

But I got to Portugal. It all happened quite quickly, though the negotiations seemed indefinitely protracted. Even so I am still on approval and expenses only.

Some kind friends, aware of my plight, invited me to a party which had a Rifle Brigade flavour. The first person I met there was Bunny Roger who must have been the most unusual officer the Regiment has ever known. When we first came to the training battalion at Tidworth as pink-faced young subalterns (Bunny used a little rouge), we were put in the charge of a fire-eating major who had recently been wounded at Calais. To him new subalterns were things to be made a meal of even after a good breakfast, and it was usually just at this time on winter mornings that he would have us out on a windy hill-top to give us the benefit of his views. On one such morning he stood before us on the crest of Sidbury Hill with all the sky around him. He wore old but beautifully polished field-boots, a scarf nonchalantly thrown round his neck and his red hair and moustaches flamed in the wind as he blazed away at us. Most of us were cringing and shivering with cold and fright, but patently Bunny was not of our number. At the end of a long and vituperative blast from the major, calculated to cut the largest ego down to size, Bunny turned to me and said in a loud stage whisper, 'Don't you *adore* his shabby finery?'

Bunny, after a distinguished career as, I think, Battalion Salvage Officer, eventually saw action in Italy where he was wounded. He then retired from the Service to set up in the *haute couture* business. The other day, out walking in Knightsbridge, he was accosted by a truck-load of ill-mannered troopers from the Horse barracks who started shouting 'Fairy, fairy', at him as they went past. They did not know, poor fools, that they were addressing an old soldier. Bunny was instantly in control. Raising a pencil-slim umbrella he said, 'If I am a fairy, this is my wand. Pouff! Be gone!'

But Bunny is a little beside the point. The person who altered my life at this party was Clare Waters, the widow of another Rifleman whom I had never met. The Waters family have an interest in a wine shipping business in the City, and owing to the death of Clare's husband, there is room for somebody else in the business. Would I be interested? One quick flash-back to the days of doctoring sour Algerian wine and my mind was made up.

There followed many anxious weeks of negotiation with another partner who, since I have no money whatsoever, saw no reason at all why I should be taken on. But I was, albeit on threadbare terms, and here I am.

> *'Shipped, by the Grace of God, in Good Order and well-conditioned, by Charles Page, in and upon the good ship called the Oporto whereof is Master, under God, for this present Voyage, Josh. Covey and now riding at Anchor in the River Thames and by God's Grace, bound for Oporto, to be delivered in the like good Order and well-conditioned at the aforesaid Port of Oporto. . . .'*

Oporto stands on a hill above the Douro and watches the river's yellow flood sluice past the anchored fishing fleet and out into the Atlantic. Looking south across the river, the town seems permanently poised in the act of poking fun at a bridge, built in a moment of aberration by old Eiffel, which connects it precariously with the Vila Nova de Gaia on the other side. Gaia is to Oporto as Pest is to Buda and it is there that my place of business is to be for the next few months to come.

> *'. . . (the Act of God, the King's Enemies, Fire and All the Every other Dangers and Accidents of the Sea, Rivers, and Navigations of whatever Nature and Kind Soever excepted) unto Mefs. Page, Noble and Co. or to their assigns; he or they*

paying Freight for the said Goods in London –
Eight pounds Nineteen shillings and four-
pence with Primage and Average accustomed.
In witness thereof, I the said Master or
Purser, of the said . . . etc, etc.
And so God send the good Ship to her
desired Port in Safety – Amen.'

So once more we begin at the bottom, or the top, depending on the way you look at it.

I have been handed over to a family called Symington whose kindness and hospitality seem inexhaustible. Their business concerns them with two of the great port wine houses, Warre's and Dows, and it is to them that I am temporarily apprenticed.

Oporto has an English colony almost entirely occupied with the port trade. These wine shippers have their own Factory House (trading house of the 'factors') to which extra-territorial rights were granted as a friendly gesture by Portugal during the Peninsular War. The Factory House, apart from an eighteenth-century nobility of structure, has one – or rather, two – remarkable features. These are twin dining-rooms, identically furnished, connected by wide double doors. Their purpose is an example of the 'big thinking' of the day. It is to enable the assembled company to abandoned at a meal's end its debris and to move next door for dessert and port wine. But of the Factory more later.

The port wine shipping community is like many other British colonies in the world. Though many speak Portuguese out of necessity, few ever marry Portuguese or indeed have close social relations with them. In fact they are much inclined to run up the Union Jack outside their lodges on every possible (British) occasion. At the same time they are hospitable and friendly people who lead comfortable, respectable, and respected lives enjoying the amenities of a place in the sun. And why not?

Socially there is a general atmosphere of 'Anyone for tennis?' and since, of course, they have their own sports club, there are frequent cries of 'Anyone for cricket?' too. Having personally always regarded a game as a pastime and not a reversion to atavism, I responded to the cry one day and disgraced myself and embarrassed everyone else by bowling four 'no-balls' in one over.

I partly reinstated myself later. It was a Factory House lunch day. We started with cold local sea-fish and mayonnaise with which we drank a white Amarante, light and dry. This was followed by mountain lamb with a local red Daō. The pudding was a Surprise Mocha followed by an excellent *serra* (mountain) cheese made from ewes' milk which, at its best, is not inferior to Port Salut. The port decanters then appeared: first the finest old tawny, and then the vintage, Warre's 1922.

We left the table at about half-past three and I was just wondering where I could go to have a *siesta* when someone said to me, 'You were at Eton, weren't you? Come and play fives.' When we got to the fives court the concrete walls were throbbing in the white heat of a southern afternoon, too hot to touch with the bare hand. After the first rally the Warre's '22 was bursting in my head in a series of blood-red explosions. I don't know how I managed to see the ball at all but I did and as far as I can remember my partner and I won the game.

My days are spent with Michael Symington who, like myself, is just out of the army. Together we are beginning to study the manufacture and exportation of this artefact called Port under the kindly tutelage of his father and twin uncles.

Each morning we report to the sample-room where, as an elementary exercise, we are taught to distinguish young wines from old. Later we are shown every variety of wine and brandy that goes to make the famous product as it is shipped to the British and other foreign markets.

The Lodges are long low buildings with earthen floors containing the huge wooden vats in which the wines are stored and blended. The smell of the lodges, being neither sweet nor sour, but a pot-pourri of red wine, oakwood and moist earth, is an olfactory museum piece; one of life's surprising bonuses.

Here we taste samples which the *capatas* draws off with a long valinch, and I have learnt without much difficulty the technique of spitting in a clean jet on to the damp earth floor. The largest vat holds over 27,000 gallons. Another, not much smaller, held a mark of wine at one time much favoured by a certain London merchant. When cleaning out this vat on one occasion they found at the bottom of it a small human skeleton, later identified as one of the workman's children who had been missing for some time. The family must have grieved for a while, but fortunately the poor man had plenty more children. The wine did not lose its popularity. Within weeks of the discovery (kept secret in Oporto) the London merchant was writing to order more, saying that the wine gave great satisfaction to his customers who appreciated it for being so fruity and 'full of body'.

Near the Lodges is the cooperage and all day long there comes from it a musical syncopation of hammers on wood. A well-made pipe will hold in the gentle swelling of its belly 115 gallons of wine and will not leak one drop. On the flat head of each finished cask a man with a calipered tool scribes the mark or designation of the wine it is to contain with quick strokes in fine English copper-plate. It is said that he can neither read nor write in his own language.

*　　*　　*

The valley of the Douro, where the vines grow in hundreds of thousands of terraces carved out of the schistous rock of the hill-side, has a cubistic beauty which appeals to me both as a would-be painter and a one-time infantryman. Through this patterned landscape the muddy river flows swiftly down from Spain (loaded, as the Portuguese say, with Spanish excrement), cutting its way through gorges where wolves still breed and golden eagles nest. Down the khaki torrent foolhardy navigators shoot rapid after rapid, steering their lovely boats with an immense stern oar, risking life, limb and cargo (wine), happy in the knowledge that God puts his hand under drunks, children and Portuguese boatmen.

The Symingtons are Catholics and it is perhaps their catholicity, in the widest sense of the word, which makes them so appreciative of the country, the language and the people of Portugal. Of their goodness they have shown me much that is of interest in northern Portugal and I have spent many appreciative hours listening to their stories of the Portuguese and enjoying their translations of native epigrams and apophthegms.

Recently I have visited with them their *quintas* both at Bomfim and Nossa Senhora da Ribeira[1] where in the middle of their vineyards they have comfortable, but not luxurious, country houses set in wild mountain scenery.

The night before we returned to Oporto they declared it to be 'a time for dance'. It took place in a flagged courtyard overhung with sweet-smelling wisteria.

The workers came in straight from the vine terraces (it is the time of the *cava*, or hoeing) smelling of olive oil, *consumo*[2] and sweat. The musicians, two young men, are both guitar players, tenor and bass respectively. Many of the dances are round dances, jerky but with a catchy rhythm that mostly start with the women singing a high-pitched nasal chant before swinging suddenly into movement.

Between numbers the *Casero*[3] goes round with a watering-can full of *consumo* which he dishes out to each person in turn in a measured pot. This *pinga*, as it is called, is drunk down in one draught by men and women alike. Anything left in the can goes to the fiddlers to give more power to their elbows.

Other dances are danced two and two, and then it is the privilege of women to invite the men. To my delight the prettiest girl in the place came and asked me and, after a few false starts, I soon got into it and was happily hopping and skipping along with this girl in a warm clinch. From time to time the more romantically inclined climbed the stairs of the courtyard and shook the trellis so that the petals of the wisteria fell like purple snowflakes on the dancers below.

Eventually Maurice Symington ordered the final *pinga* to indicate that the entertainment was at a close. At the end the *Casero* called for a cheer for the family and all joined in with an animated '*Viva Patroes!*' Feudalism, perhaps, but how benign!

* * *

The time has come to move on and I take a last walk through Gaia. The narrow streets are built of huge granite blocks worn

---

[1] Our Lady of the Ford.
[2] Wine made from the second pressing of the grapes.
[3] Manager of the House and Lodges.

into ruts by the wheels of the bullock-carts which have been taking the port casks down to the quayside for more than a century. The English names outside the lodges – Cockburn, Taylor Fladgate and Yeatman, MacKenzie, Hunt Roope, Sandeman, Warre – which at first seemed so incongruous in this Latin setting, now seem an unalterable part of the scene.

I pass the usual barefoot women carrying baskets of empty bottles on their heads and follow an ox-cart loaded with pipes and hogheads. The two waggoners are walking one behind the other. The last one obviously has caught a cold because I watch him pull out the tail of his companion's shirt and blow his nose on it. Having done so, he stuffs it back inside the other's breeches without the exchange of a by-your-leave or a word of protest.

★   ★   ★

'Lisbõa – Badajoz – Sevilla.' The Lusitania Express swishes through the night while I sit in the Edwardian comfort of the restaurant car dosing myself with brandy against the *grippe*. The passport and customs officials visit me in turn and then sit down just behind me for their own dinner – soup, lemon sole and new potatoes, creamed chicken and rice, more rice, more chicken, plenty of *vinho de casa*, some sort of pudding, cheese – plenty of cheese – fruit – plenty of fruit. Silently they worked their way through the long menu. Did I say silently? No, the sound of their mastication is like hands gently clapping in wet shammy-leather gloves. I wish I could tuck in too, but I am feverish and can only manage a little fish to oblige the waiter.

We stop at some dark and nameless station and the conductor gets out to shake hands with the station-master under the only oil lamp. Beyond the light the *grillos* fill the silence, playing their 'cello legs in vibrant diapason. Then the train pulls out, puffing slowly in time to the station-master's retreating footsteps.

Later half a moon breaks through a mackerel sky revealing the soft shapes of cork and olive trees. Soon we will be in Spain.

Morning and Jerez-de-la-Frontera; white walls of Spain, indigo sky and purple bougainvillaea. There are storks clacking on every roof-top and the streets are full of brown men in

Cordoban hats carrying heavy-ended sticks. The music of de Falla did not tell a lie.

I have been three days in bed at the Los Cisnes with galloping diarrhoea and a fever. A doctor has been and gone but since we have no word of any language in common I doubt if much good will come of it. Friendly house-maids also come and go, to look and laugh at the phenomenon of *un Señorito Ingles* in bed. They try to coax me to eat but I cannot. I just lie there in the white-washed room aware of the brilliant sun outside and read – what? *The Pickwick Papers*, and wait for my troubles to go. It is the time of the *feria* and I am desperate to go out and get the feel of this place which, from the moment of hearing those first bars of music in the Victoria and Albert Museum, I knew.

Mauricio Gonzalez is one of a number of *Jerezanos* whose surnames, linked in perpetuity to brands of sherry, are variously Domecq, Osborne, Gordon and Garvey, and permutations of all of them. Their English is as immaculate as English nannies and a Downside or Ampleforth education can make it. Encouraged by Mauricio's kindly persuasion I drag myself out of bed to attend the *Corrida de Toros*.

It had already started by the time we reached the bull-ring. It was all so matter-of-fact as we began to climb the cool white stairs of the *sombra* up to the Gonzalez box. When we emerged at the top it was as if a grey gauze was being lifted. There suddenly was the most brilliant spectacle that I have ever yet seen, and I knew at that moment that bull-fighting was going to be my obsession for many years to come.

I do not remember much of this *corrida*, and yet in a sense I remember everything. It is divided in my mind between the elegant restraint of well-dressed ladies and gentlemen in the *sombra*, and shouts, flies and orange-peel in the *sol*. The arena itself is half-eclipsed by shadow, one side blue-grey and the other yellow and scarlet, fierce as the Spanish flag.

I sit next to the eldest Gonzalez girl, who has dark eyes, black hair and a white skin. Her name, Maria-Decia, is as coolly elegant as she is. Further down is her younger sister who has rosy-brown colouring and thick fair hair in a loose bun.

Now a phlegmy trumpet brasses forth and a pale young man with a gentle face doffs his hat and makes a formal bow. I become aware of Maria-Decia talking to me.

'I apologize that my sister and I are not got up properly for the occasion, but one has to have one's hair done specially to wear a *mantilla* and it is a bit of a bore.'

I murmur something appropriate and try as far as politeness will allow to turn my attention back to the ring. But by now Mauricio, chatting gaily to friends in a neighbouring box, is pouring out some sherry and this too requires my polite attention.

As we sip our wine out of elegant *copitas,* vendors of drinks in the *sol* shout their wares in voices like ground glass while their clients drink thirstily out of the necks of bottles.

Maria-Decia murmurs something about the difficulty of getting hold of a hairdresser in *Feria* week, and I get a glimpse of the pale matador lying face down in the sand. A quartet of grey-green men flap magenta capes under the bull's nose, and the *sol* half-rises to its feet. Gouts of viscous crimson pump out of the hole in the bull's back and flow down his black flanks. His stiff tongue sticks out grey and dry as a lavender-bag, but that too becomes suddenly and shockingly red when a sword penetrates a lung. Above it all a phalanx of the Civil Guard, green-garbed, green-jowled and detached, remain decorously seated.

'I haven't seen a decent bull-fight in thirty years,' says old Mr Williams from the neighbouring box.

'I think they shave the horns these days,' Maria-Decia says.

The matador is afoot once more, poised, sword pointed, tremulous, waiting. There is a sudden hush as the man and the bull meet, touch, and join together for a brief moment of time. When they part there is nothing to be seen of the sword except its red hilt in the bull's hump. The young man raises his left hand in an imperious gesture and the bull goes slowly down one knee at a time like an old man to prayer. Then comes a fanfare and much cracking of whips as a gaily caparisoned three-in-hand of mules drags out the limp carcass to the cheers and counter-cheers of the crowd.

I am feeling very weak. I have not been able to take any proper food for days. But sherry is very nourishing and by keeping it flowing through my veins I am able to steer my way through this geranium night of *fiesta* with its palms and fireworks, horse-droppings and carnations, spit, pips, beggars and prawnshells, and brown fingers, and gypsies' windpipes, and untouchable girls in the darkness of the star-pocked, moon-drunk night.

IO

The subsequent stages of Peter Luke's wine trade apprenticeship took him to the Rioja district: Haro, Logroño and Bilbao. He then crossed the Irun-Hendaye frontier to get to Bordeaux. Here he briefly records his impressions.

*   *   *

Bordeaux is the *fons et origo* of provincial snobbery and you don't have to read Mauriac to find it out. The smart ladies of this city wear self-conscious hats for almost all occasions including night-time entertainments. When they don't wear hats – and sometimes even when they do – they wear tartan because most of them will drum up a Scottish ancestor from somewhere. It does not need much familiarity with the French language to know how funny names such as Farquhar and Monroe and MacMahon sound at the tip of a Gallic tongue. Moreover, at all forms of socializing – at the equivalent of cocktail parties, for example – one is introduced to, and has to shake hands with, all present. If therefore there are sixty guests and one gives two shakes to each hand, that comes to a hundred and twenty shakes which is enough to give anybody tennis-elbow. At one such cocktail party I was given young vintage port to drink, but that was an enormous *gaffe* and one which my hostess was not allowed to forget.

To be able to compete for social recognition, a Bordelais needs to have an English, Scottish or Irish surname. In default of this, an English Christian or nick-name will do. He also does well to have an English accent, an English university education and, of course, an English tailor. It helps, too, to be a hunting man (they hunt roebuck and wild boar in the Landes) in which case your man will buy his saddles from England although they make perfectly good ones in France. One man I know secretly keeps a bowler hat in London to wear on visits there. All ladies from Bordeaux on a visit to London make straight for the

Scotch House in Knightsbridge in order to stock up with tartan.

Perhaps one of the finer points of Bordeaux snobbery is to be, if possible, a Protestant. Failing that, one can always be a Monarchist, but this is almost too easy.

But the great paradox about the Bordelais is that while apeing the English they also despise them, presumably because they are not French. So you see, as snobs, they are invincible. I only once managed to put down a Bordelais and that was in Ireland where I was playing on home ground, as it were. Of this more later.

But there are two men in Bordeaux whom I absolve unequivocally from all accusation of snobbery. One is called Peyrelongue, a Gascon, and the other is a Barton from Ireland.

★   ★   ★

From Bordeaux Luke went to the Côte d'Or of Burgundy, then to Cognac in the Charante, and finally to the champagne district of Rheims and Epernay. These stages were neither more, nor less, interesting than the wines he tasted and the food he ate, and a chronicle of them would not be relevant here. What at this time he did not understand, though perhaps he vaguely sensed it, was that the pursuit of a career in the wine trade in England is no different from the pursuit of any other commercial enterprise. 'Always remember, Luke,' said his managing director to him one day in the lavatory, 'wine is a commodity.'

On return to England, therefore, Luke found himself to some extent equipped to discuss the merits and demerits of fine wine, but he was no more prepared or qualified to become a commercial traveller – which was effectively to be his rôle – than he had been to become a sub-editor on Reuter's news desk. Nevertheless, this was to be his life for the next nine years.

Early days in the City, therefore, were not too promising when it was discovered that neither he nor his managing director had come to a mutual understanding as to what the job was really about. The job was really about sales figures and margins of profit.

Aside from this, he was at intervals struck down with sudden and violent attacks of diarrhoea together with short periods of losing consciousness. An electro-cardiograph proved negative. But one day, in prompt response to a summons, a doctor caught Luke in the act of passing out. He stuck an adrenalin needle straight into the most available part of his anatomy, the bony part of the chest, and carried him up to bed.

Then after careful thought and study, Dr Montague Rawkins produced a diagnosis which probably saved Peter Luke's life. The patient was suffering from heart-block caused, he concluded, by acute amoebic hepatitis occasioned by amoebic dysentery first contracted in the Western Desert five years before and, owing to the exigences of the service, never treated at the time.

The cure, Rawkins decided, was to kill the amoeba with a drug called Emetine, then the other conditions would cure themselves. The diagnosis was correct, but the cure took nearly two years.

Luke's narrative resumes. . . .

★   ★   ★

It is very strange to be about to die at the age of twenty-eight. I have nearly been killed a hundred times but I have never before been face to face with death. For the benefit of aficionados, therefore, I will tell you what heart-block is, or rather, what it does. It makes your heart miss beats. It can miss one, two, three, four, five or even six beats, by which time you pass out. In other words the heart stops beating. Then, maybe, it starts again. But if it doesn't – then you are dead, aren't you?

So simple. It is a sort of cat-and-mouse game with the Grim Reaper playing Pussy. I find myself trotting out clichés like, 'I'm too young to die.' And then, instead of feeling sorry for myself, I feel overwhelmed with sadness for all those who will miss me after I have gone.

The Emetine treatment requires the patient to be subjected to a course of injections at intervals extending over a period of up to two years. Each course consists of seven injections, one each day. This is nothing in itself, but unfortunately Emetine is a depressant. Shots one and two are all right, but by about shot four one becomes thoroughly miserable and, after shot five, I for one am so reduced that I cannot bear to read even the lightest book.

That is how I took to betting on horses. The operation of it is so simple, and the excitement serves to some extent to counter the depression caused by the injections. The only equipment required is a telephone, a radio, a bookmaker and a few mid-day papers.

I notice, however, that as time goes on my betting is becoming more sophisticated. I now subscribe to *Raceform*, *Chaseform* and *Sporting Weekly*. Further, my bets have become more mature. Five bob each way has now become twenty quid to win. Alternatively I work out elaborate mixed doubles and accumulators, or play the game of backing odds-on favourites for a place on the Tote.

Emetine is a non-habit-forming drug. I don't know about racing. Unfortunately the whole business has boomeranged on Lettice. She has kindly undertaken to give me the injections, and she does it very well. This saves the doctor's bills, but the more she pumps Emetine into me, the more I bet on horses, and this causes her much anxiety. Rightly so. We have no money except the temporary army pension I draw because of the dysentery. She should not of course have married me in the first place, but she can hardly be blamed for that.

Last night I dreamt that I was shot through the left forearm by bullets from a machine-gun. I amputated my hand myself and grafted a new one on to the stump. It was rather a neat job but in the process I lost a gold ring I usually wear which belonged to my grandfather. I woke up with a rheumaticky ache in my arm. This, I believe, is another side-effect to Emetine. But at least I am not now going to die.

II

'Good night, Mr Wewds.'

I was adjusting my dress in conformity with regulations on the steps of the Sydney Street Gents. The voice seemed to come from above.

'Good night, Mr Wewds.' The voice again, this time with more decibels and a touch of *vibrato*. I can now see that it comes from an old girl peering down from street level. A subterranean rumble acknowledges the farewell.

'Naht.'

That must be Woods I thought, and the old tot must be the drip-dauber from the Ladies next door.

'See yer tomorrer,' she yells.

'Raht.'

So Mr Pyramus Woods and Mrs Thisbe have a relationship. 'See yer tomorrer then,' she lets rip once more out of the night. This time no response from below save the borborygmus of a plug.

'Wall, that vile Wall which did these lovers sunder. . . .'

Too shiny for grafiti, I study its advertisements while buttoning the last fly. Where do flies go in the winter time?

DELAY IS DANGEROUS

And old Scrotum the wrinkled retainer?

CAN BE CURED IF TREATED EARLY

Mr Woods appears mop in hand from below, British bulldog, *circa* 1914, 'Old Contemptible' down to the brass stud of his collarless shirt. After a few passes with the sparse and obscene mop he looks up.

'Yer?' he asks aggressively.

'I was just reading your ads.'

'It says no loiterin'.'

'How else can one read them then?'

139

'I'm locking up now it's after time.'

Upstairs in the dark it has stopped raining but the traffic lights at the junction of Sydney Street and the Kings Road set colourful reflections dancing across the wet tarmac.

I head for home. The streets are darkish and empty. I turn right at Cale Street, pass Pond Place and on into Mossop Street, enjoying the solitude and listening with satisfaction to my footsteps on the empty pavement.

Brother Michael has his problems, but they are very different from my own. When I flew the coop at the age of eighteen he became a sort of only child. And when our mother and father, who had spent nearly thirty years of mutual hatred together 'for the sake of the children', finally decided to give it up, he was the baby left holding the parents. After five years of persecution at Eton – according to him, as reprisal for offences previously committed by me – he followed me into the Rifle Brigade. Then just when he was about to go abroad to join a service Battalion he had a fall during training and was medically down-graded. Thereafter, until the end of the war, he led perforce a purposeless, demoralizing existence, getting into one military scrape after another. Meanwhile I was abroad leading what was then considered to be a glamorous sort of life culminating with my having a medal pinned on my chest in the field by Field-Marshal Montgomery; a state of affairs well designed to exacerbate any manifestations of Younger Brother Complex that might have existed.

On – or possibly before – demobilization, however, Michael gradually came into the periphery of the London literati, both of the *haute*- and *demi-monde*. By the time that I had contracted what he called a 'bourgeois marriage' (Lettice being of the Landed Gentry) and had acquired a truly bourgeois job, our rôles were sharply and palpably reversed. And so they remain today, with Mick as the top half of Byron and me as his Lordship's limp.

I let myself into the house and turn on the light. On the table are several letters, most of them in brown manilla envelopes with flaps tucked in. The registered one I can see is from the landlord about the rent. There is a dog's mess on the carpet. My elation is quickly gone and I feel myself trapped in a triangle between the landlord's letter, the dog's mess and my wife. I hope she is asleep.

I get undressed and go into the bedroom. The light is on between the beds and only the top of a hair-net is visible above the bedclothes.

She stirs and murmurs sleepily, 'Did you lock the front door?'

'Yes.'

'. . . and put out the hall light?'

'Yes, I always do.'

I am afraid she is beginning to wake up.

'Had a good party?'

'It was hardly a party.'

I pick up a book not too hopefully: Hardy's *Dynasts*.

'It must have been a good enough party to keep you up all night.'

'Hardly all night. It's just after eleven.'

'Or was there some other attraction?' Her voice is less sleepy now.

'If you call Mick some other attraction. . . . Incidentally the dog has made a mess on the carpet.'

I turn my back and try to read:

> *'It looks as if this doughty coalition*
> *on which we have lavished so much pay and pains*
> *would end in wreck. . . .'*

but rising anger thwarts comprehension.

Mick and I had met at the Goat and Compass and had had some food and beer. Not that either of us like pubs or beer much but it was mutual territory in a working-class environment where one could talk in peace.

But now she had got the wind under her tail.

'I always know when you have been out with Micky by your sulky looks. Why are you so influenced by Micky?'

'I'm not influenced by Mick. I just like his company and I think he likes mine. If there is any "influence" it is probably mutual which is not a bad thing.'

A pause, then: 'He is absolutely rotten and you know it. People like Micky ought to be sent down a coal mine.'

I try a joke: 'I don't think that would help the coal industry much.'

'Why doesn't he get a job then?'

'I'm trying to read.'

'Well why doesn't he?'

'I'm trying to read.'

'You can't answer that question can you?'

All too easily provoked, I lower my book and twist my neck round to answer back. 'If you want to know, he values his freedom too much.'

Fool, now I've really let myself in for it.

'What? Do you mean to say that any young man who "values his freedom", as you put it, needn't work?'

'Of course I don't mean that. I mean that a man who has some sort of talent like Mick shouldn't bind himself to any old form of drudgery while he can still explore the possibilities of using his talent to advantage.'

'In the meantime he is quite content to sponge on his family, and you, and anybody else who is fool enough to lend him money or stand him a good dinner.'

'There is no rule that I am aware of against lending one's brother ten bob or standing him an occasional meal, is there?'

'What good is he to anybody, I'd like to know.'

'Mick is an intelligent human being who has no responsibilities. His private life is no concern of mine except from a purely academic point of view.'

'Academic! I always know when you've been out with him by the way you talk. Mick is an absolute sponger. He doesn't give a damn for you or anybody else, and you know it. I'd rather you didn't bring him to the house any more. I don't want him near the children.'

'That's an absurd statement to make, and you've no right to make it.'

She turns over in emphatic silence. I look for the place in my book but can't find it. My anger, mounting in beats, makes concentration impossible. I chuck Hardy on the floor and switch off the light. In the darkness black flashes of hate pulse back and forth between the single beds.

After a while I calm down but cannot get to sleep. Sleepless nights have some advantages, however unpleasant they may be.

One can think clearly, even creatively, sometimes. I begin to see all too clearly my predicament. I have signed a contract with a 'no-escape' clause, and worse: I have committed two hostages to fortune to make it binding forever. Woe is bloody me!

Apart from anything else, what the hell have I become? A contemptible hybrid and no longer my own man at all. Since my marriage I have become of all things the possessor of a bowler hat, a dozen stiff collars, and an umbrella with my name on it. Add to that a couple of dark suits bought on tick from Welsh and Geoffreys, the regimental tailor, in which garb of shame I go to the City every morning, dreading lest I may run into Mick or some of our Bohemian friends. Already Nanos Valaoritis[1] has made disparaging remarks about my 'bourgeois' collars, and Robert Kee[2] says I look like one of the Forsytes. I suppose I do: Soames to the life. Conversely, on days or evenings off, I am apprehensive about running into my (perfectly amiable) City friends when I am with the *louche* but stimulating company that I prefer to keep. So I am leading two thoroughly unsatisfactory lives – or one doubly unsatisfactory double-life – and have no identity of my own. How perfectly ghastly. Would I, I wonder, ever hold a woman I love in my arms again? Highly improbable. And what chances of ever returning to the Mediterranean? In the foreseeable future, none. In my despair, these two quite unrelated matters are my screaming *cries du coeur*.

I remember the time when Phoebe and I went down to the Côte d'Azure from Paris. Third-class train, of course. At some time during the night, though, we found we had the compartment to ourselves and managed to get ourselves into a favourable clinch. We were still in it, *flagrante delicto*, when the delighted conductor woke us in the morning. After enthusing about the raptures of young love, he became equally eloquent about the beauties of the Midi. At his suggestion we looked out of the window and saw that the country had quite changed overnight. We were now in the land of the olive and the cypress and the prickly-pear and I never wanted to be anywhere else again.

At Marseilles we lunched at a restaurant in the Vieux Port

[1] Greek poet.
[2] English writer.

near where the boats take off for the Château d'If. It could have been owned by Raimu for all I knew. I do not remember at all what we ate. I only recollect as if it were the day before yesterday the utter perfection of the ambience: the smells of saffron, of frying olive oil, of fresh fish cooking; sun on the water, sun through a bright coloured awning, sun transmogrifying me through a litre of pink Midi wine. I felt absolutely drunk, but I was drunk with the sun in my head not the wine in my belly.

Later we took the coastal train and got out, I think, at the first stop. It was a little fishing port called Cassis. There we swam naked in a *calanque* and later drank *pastis* watching the moon come up over Cap Canaille. Not in itself an unusual sort of idyll, but one that in these depressing circumstances means much to me now. If the Mediterranean is not in my blood, it is certainly in my heart and in my understanding, and I shall never be able to live happily anywhere else.

I suppose I drifted off to sleep because I dreamt I was in bed making love to X's wife who is rather beautiful in a pre-Raphaelite sort of way. Unfortunately X came in and was very angry which is not at all like him in real life. However, by dint of great physical effort, and by exerting an enormous amount of will-power, I managed by beating my arms very, very hard to fly away. I can always fly away in dreams if I make a strong enough effort of will. The take-off is sometimes rather difficult but once off the ground I can fly, soar, hover and glide for as long as I like.

Now I can hear the hideous whingeing of the milkman's van. If he rings the bell I, who have seen so many nobler dawns, will have to get up and pay him. It is still dark outside. Do I really deserve this? Oh God, what wouldn't I give for a shot of 'gun-fire' now!

12

One January day Miss Molloy was walking down the Mall in Cork City minding her business. Somewhere between Morrison's Island and the County Club she found her way obstructed by an impenetrable wall of Donegal tweed. Looking up at this sky-scraper of brown wool, which smelt of sheep's urine, bacon fat and jelly-babies, she saw somewhere near the top a large purple face, if indeed it was a face. On further inspection it did appear to be a face because it had a long and angry-looking nose, and the nose was running. Yes, and the whole structure, now swaying slightly, was surmounted by something small, round and greenish which obviously served as a hat. Had she encountered a monster?

Miss Molloy sought to circumnavigate the terrifying obstacle but could not. Petrified, she watched a purple hand the size of a Limerick ham emerge from some cavern in the Donegal tweed, raise itself slowly to the face, and remove an obstruction from the face's mouth. This obstruction, sodden with saliva, was un-doubtedly a black Burma cheroot. Then like Moses from the mountain-top the voice spake. What is more it spake to Miss Molloy.

'Madam, have you a match?' the voice, like a faulty loud-speaker, crackled and boomed. Only too willing to appease the monster, Miss Molloy scrabbled in the bottom of her little black bag. Jesus, Mary and Joseph, Blessed St Anthony, please let me find a match. If not what terrible tribute will this creature demand? A whole sodality of Irish Virgins, surely.

Ah, thanks be to God, here we are now. Wedged in amongst the fluff and debris at the bottom of the bag lay one Swan Vesta. Miss Molloy proffered it at trembling arm's length.

'And what in God's name am I supposed to do with that?' roared the awful voice. 'Strike it on my arse?' But Miss Molloy, having seen a break in the traffic, had scuttled across the road.

Fitz, or to give him his full style, Major-General Gerald Fitzgerald, CBE, MC, retd, and now of Aghavrin House, Macroom,

Co. Cork, is rumoured to be my godfather though I have never had any confirmation of this, nor have I seen any manifestation of it beyond the fact that he dragged me off one Sunday to the Parish Church (of Ireland) at Carrigadrohid. We were the only members of the congregation and the parson took for the text of his sermon 'evil-speaking, lying and slandering'. Under the cirumstances Fitz took it personally and from then on gave his miniscule oblation to the RC priest instead, who abused him to his face but did not preach sermons at him.

Fitz is the largest man in Ireland except Big Bill Dean, the wrestler. I know because I measured them back to back in the lobby of the Imperial Hotel in Cork. They are both six foot seven.

Fitz is a bachelor. Apparently he did once contemplate getting married. The object of this intention was the daughter of his old friend, the Comte de Gironde. I asked him if he had actually proposed.

'Yes,' he replied.

'What did she say?'

'No.'

So now rumour has it that I am his heir, but heir to what, I ask myself. In any case it is *I* who keep *him* - at least in wine, sweets and cigars.

One thing Fitz has done for me, albeit indirectly, is to secure Ireland for me as my business bailliwick. When my managing director heard that I had vague connexions with Ireland he lost no time in sending me there. For one thing, though the firm is a Catholic one and has a good trade in Ireland (mainly claret and altar wine), he did not want to go there himself. Later I found out why. He is a Scot and had been in the country as a British officer during the Troubles. Who knows but that even now someone isn't waiting for him behind a hedge with a bullet. There is only one thing more calculated to provoke than setting Moors against Spaniards, and that is putting the Irish down with Galloglasses.

The arrangement suits me very well, of course, particularly in view of the sad state of my marital relations. In addition, since business often takes me to Cork, I see quite a bit of 'the Gineral' which I enjoy.

Fitz used to be in the Indian Army. He was gazetted to Fane's

Horse (19th Cavalry), and became a bosom pal of my grandfather, Jim Fremlin, who was in the same regiment. During the First World War some genius had the bright idea of bringing the Indian Cavalry over to fight in the trenches of Flanders. The French liaison officer to the regiment at the time was a young man known in private life as the Comte de Gironde. My grandfather could speak a bit of Urdu, Pushtu, Tamil and Hindustani, but Fitz enjoyed speaking French. He and De Gironde palled up and Fitz has been a francophil ever since.

My grandfather, as soon as the war was over, went back to India where, in 1926, he died as a result of being mauled by a bear – or rather two bears. They were fighting together and my grandfather, in order to get a clear shot at one of them, kicked the other in the backside. It was a classic lesson in how not to interfere in other people's quarrels because both bears then turned on him and gave him his *quietus*. Evelyn Waugh once wrote that he (Jim Fremlin) had been eaten by a tiger. He was misinformed, possibly by my Uncle Rupert, who may have been tempted to embellish the story of his father's demise.

Fitz is a legend in his own time and one that belongs strictly to the Anglo-Irish world of Somerville and Ross. In fact he knew Admiral Somerville, and possibly the ladies too, though I keep on forgetting to ask him about them. During the Second World War he held a non-operational command in India, and at the end of it retired to his home in Co. Cork.

To a man born into the Protestant ascendancy towards the end of the nineteenth century, and who had lived most of his life abroad, Ireland in 1946 must have seemed a strange place. By this time the 'ascendancy' had quite been taken out of Protestantism and the world described by Edith Somerville and Violet Martin (Martin Ross) was gone for ever. Many would say 'a good job too'.

The day that Fitz returned to his native land was a Friday. He disembarked from the *Inishfallen* at Cork on a wet and windy morning and made straight for the County Club in search of warmth and breakfast. He visualized a roaring fire and a sideboard of silver dishes sizzling with sausages, eggs and rashers, and kidneys plus a little cold ham, perhaps, to fill the gaps. But things are seldom as you expect to find them in Ireland. In the first place he had trouble in gaining admittance. The night porter, who had drunk deep the night before, was sleeping even deeper on this particular morning. Secondly, the sods of damp turf which the maid had laid in the large Georgian fireplace defied ignition.

Even so, the General did not quite realize how times had changed until he asked for his breakfast. Mary, the maid on duty, was a country girl, new to service, and one who had hardly seen a Protestant in her life until the moment she was confronted with the General. To his demand, 'Where is my breakfast?' her reply was another question (it being Friday): 'Are ye fasting?'

Fitz's answer is alleged to have been heard in Poona.

At Aghavrin I found Fitz in an armchair absorbed in his usual literary diet, an old Army List.

'Do you realize,' he said without a greeting, 'that old Smiley had not passed Staff College in 1913? Have you got a cigar?'

'No, General, I am sorry.'

'Got any petrol in that car of yours?'

I said I had.

'All right, we can drive into Macroom and buy one.'

By the time we got to Macroom it was about ten at night. But this did not deter Fitz who battered on the tobacconist's doors and windows until the old lady who owned the shop came down.

'Glory be to God, didn't you put the heart across me, and there was I thinking it was the Antichrist himself knocking on the door, and it was only yourself, Gineral dear.'

In fact the old lady was far more frightened of the Black and Tans than of the Antichrist, or perhaps she thought they were one and the same. At all events so relieved was she to see the General that she sold him – or rather me – a cigar for half-price because it had been in the shop since Christmas.

'Tomorrow we will go shooting,' he said outside, trying to light the thing. I replied that I could not because I had business to do in town.

'Business?' he said disdainfully. 'Gentlemen don't do business.'

We went shooting. As a matter of fact I always keep a gun and pair of gum-boots in the back of the car on top of the wine samples. I enjoy my business tours around the country and it is a good thing to get away from Dublin and cool the eye-balls a bit in the fresh air. I always take a picnic lunch with me on these trips and with it I drink the out-of-date claret samples. Somebody once said that they could trace my course round Ireland by the empty sample bottles at the side of the road.

Snipe shooting is mostly free in Ireland and whenever I pass a likely-looking bog I stop the car, put on my gum-boots, and walk it up for half an hour or so. Sometimes one is rewarded by a hare or the odd pheasant and these, plus a brace or two of snipe, always make a suitable *douceur* to any friends with whom I might be likely to stay *en route*.

A red bog is basically an area of peat on which various types of ling and heather grow giving it a rufous colour over-all. Here and there, however, there are patches of brilliant green where cresses and variegated mosses grow. These are to be avoided at all cost.

Fitz should have known better. When I first heard his shout I thought he had lost a bird and wanted me to help him look for it. I therefore did not hurry over. Only slowly did it impinge upon me that he was in some sort of trouble.

By the time I got to him he was above the knees in one of these veridian bog-holes and still sinking. My first efforts to pull him out by the hand only succeeded in making him thresh around and go deeper in. By this time we both realized that it was serious. Fitz's enormous weight plus his lack of agility made him the worst person to be in this sort of predicament. I saw the very real possibility of him disappearing like Carver Doone.

('What are your last words, General?'

'Glug, glug.')

'Fall forward,' I said. 'Try and lie flat on your stomach.'

By this time he was up to his crutch but he did fall forward, holding his gun in front of him like handle-bars, I got hold of it in the middle and started to pull. As he got flatter, so was he able, slowly and one at a time, to raise his legs up out of the bog a bit. Eventually, with him crawling and me pulling, I got him on to hard ground where we both lay gasping for breath.

Fitz likes to go to bed early even though his bed, which he shares with a Sealyham called Nelson (but pronounced as in French), is much too small for him. Once there he likes company

while he sucks jube-jubes and sings the dirty French songs which
he learnt in the 1914 war. We usually end up with a jolly chorus
that goes more or less as follows:

> *Trou de mon queue*
> *De quoi te plain-tu?*
> *N'est-tu pas bien*
> *En milieu de mon fesse?*

> *Trou de mon queue*
> *De quoi te plain-tu?*
> *N'est-tu pas bien*
> *En milieu de mon queue.*

Sometimes we have arguments. They usually begin on my
arrival when he asks me rather aggressively what keeps me in
Dublin. He can't believe there is any reason for anyone to go to
Dublin unless it is to visit the Kildare Street Club, of which I
am not a member. All the same, he always wants to know what
I have been doing.

The other day I happened to mention that I had been at a very
amusing luncheon party with the Ross-Williamson's where
Michael MacLiammóir had been present.

'Who is MacLiammóir?' says Fitz. I can tell by the way he lays
his ears back and looks out of the corners of his eyes that he
knows perfectly well, but I play along innocently.

'One of Ireland's most famous actors,' I say.

'A bit suspect, isn't he?'

'Suspect?' I am all innocence again.

'Yes, suspect.'

'Suspect of what, General?' I ask.

'Well, he's an artist, isn't he?'

'I would certainly call him an artist,' I say because I genuinely
admire MacLiammóir.

'Well all artists are suspect, aren't they?'

In order not to become involved I hedge and belittle the whole
thing so that Fitz gets bored and picks up the Army List again.

'Who did you say your Brigadier was?'

Satisfied that the Brigadier Hinde I mention was not the Hinde he knew in Jullundar, he returns to the subject of the theatrical profession.

'Did you ever see Le Grand Pêteur?' he asks.

I had to admit that I had not done so.

'De Gironde was very fond of him. Some years ago he made me go to Paris and see the feller before he got too old for the job.'

I begin to wonder who this actor was, and then I remember hearing that some time after the turn of the century there had been a music-hall artiste, if that is the word, called Le Pêtanist who had earned fame and a living on the halls by his skill at musical farting.

'And did you go and see him, General?' I asked.

'Yes,' he replied, 'but when we got there the theatre was closed. There was a notice outside saying LE GRAND PÉTEUR EST EN VACANCE.'

'Bad luck, General,' I said, 'but it must be a relief for the poor fellow to give up farting for a few weeks in the year.' He would probably enjoy a change of diet, I thought, and have a chance to lay off the haricots for a bit. But by this time the General's huge purple nose was back in the Army List.

Francophil that he was, he welcomed my suggestion that I should bring Edouard Cruse to see him, particularly since Edouard came from Bordeaux (Départment de Gironde) and is a joint-master of a pack of hounds there.

We arrived to find Fitz sitting in an armchair having his toe-nails cut by Birdie, his little maid, who lives with her grandmother down the boreen. Fitz had massacred himself shaving that morning and there was still signs of the blood which had trickled down his neck and coagulated on his collar. I saw Edouard shrink a little into his blue business suit.

'Anybody got a cigar?' Fitz roared as soon as the introductions were over.

'Sorry, General,' I said.

'Bloody man, what is the use of you?'

Edouard gathered himself up to take the strain. Knowing his mind, I could see he was reassuring himself that this Brobdingnagian figure had recently been a General in the British Army.

I was equally sure that he would be trying to work out why Fitz should have been in the British, rather than the Irish Army. The illogicalities of Ireland and, in particular, the divided loyalties of the Anglo-Irish, are usually too much for the French.

Thinking he would be on safe ground, Edouard made one or two conversational passes about horses and hunting.

'Got any petrol in that car of yours?' Fitz asks.

When I answer in the affirmative he says, 'Then we'll take Monsieur Cruse and introduce him to the local MFH. We can get a cigar on the way. Brought any wine?'

We drove up to the usual square block of Georgian 'gentleman's residence' and, led by Fitz, trooped up the front steps. The hall door was open but nobody appeared to be about. Fitz let out a few hollers and banged a brass gong. Then, picking up a hunting-horn off the hall table, he was just going to give a blast when a maid appeared. On being put to the question by Fitz she announced that the 'meejor' had gone to Cork and wouldn't be back until late. Fitz, who doesn't like to waste a journey, even in somebody else's car, announced that we would take a look round the garden. So we all trooped out again.

It is in fact a nice garden and its well-kept look was surely due to the middle-aged woman we met turning manure into a herbaceous border. She wore gum-boots, an old brown mac torn at the pocket, and talked in the sing-song accent of West Cork. She and the General chatted a while of this and that and then we went our way – but not before Edouard, who dislikes gardening, had expressed his disappointment at our failure to have met the Master of Foxhounds.

In Macroom Fitz surprised me by saying that he would go himself to the tobacconist. When he got back to the car he was holding two good-looking smokes in his hand. Once in – and getting him in is no small business – he lit up one of them and surprised Edouard by putting the other in his pocket. 'I'll keep this one for after dinner,' he said.

Having got over the shock of not being offered the second cigar (I don't smoke), Edouard once again expressed his sorrow at not having met the owners of the house that we had just visited. This was my little moment.

'Edouard, old fellow,' I said, 'that was your hostess we were speaking to in the garden just now.'

Evidently it is not easy for the French to recognize the gentry unless they wear picture-hats and tartans.

Back at Aghavrin we had a jolly evening enlivened by some port that I had taken the precaution to provide. Fitz was in good form, telling stories about De Gironde whose son, Bernard, Edouard apparently knew.

'Bernard! Even his father can't stand him,' said Fitz. And then, in an imitation of his old friend, he went on, 'Bernard, 'e ees a sheet.' Eventually we went to bed.

Upstairs Edouard and I were due to share the 'best' bedroom for the sake of the warmth which was provided by two sods of turf leaning sadly against each other and disproving the old adage that 'Where there is smoke there is fire'.

When it came to the choice of beds I played my hand coolly, knowing from experience that most of the year round the Aghavrin beds tend to be like wet sponges covered in mildew.

'Which bed will you have, Edouard?' I said heartily, pretending to feel the quality of the springs of the one nearest the fire-place. In fact I was feeling to see if by any chance Birdie had put a 'hot jar' in either of them. She had, but only in the one that I was feeling, so I casually threw my grip on top of it before Edouard could find out.

Once in our respective beds Edouard lit up a Gauloise to keep himself warm, while I lay listening to the occasional plop of water dripping from his mattress and, from across the corridor, the sound of Fitz singing a nocturne to Nelson:

> J'aime les odeurs des pieds,
> Le jaune des oreilles.
> J'aime les gros loups du nez,
> Le crachat des vielles,
> Si vous voulez m'en donner,
> Je saurai bien les manger.

But there is another Ireland, far removed from *Some Experiences of an Irish R.M.* and that is the one that slowly began to reveal itself to me. I welcomed it gratefully.

13

'Tis time at length for me to foot it homeward
for the poets of the world lie sleeping.

The quotation is a rough translation from the Irish of the seventeenth-century poet, David O'Bruadair, and the inference quite plainly is that in Ireland, then as now, the poets and the blatherskites of the world talk and drink their way through the night till they fall flat on their faces. The poet in this case – though we have only his word for it – held his liquor better than the rest since he is able to walk away from the scene with an apophthegm on his lips.

I like to think of myself as the O'Bruadair *de nos jours* and, if I am no poet, I have walked away from a good many such scenes to see dawn breaking in the sky over Dublin – and over Cork and Galway too. My companions vary and who they are tends to depend upon what I have been doing earlier in the day, but at the heel of the hunt there is nearly always Nora FitzGerald or Dudley Walsh, and very often the two of them. The talk, of course, gets cleverer and wittier as the night goes by until, suddenly, there is some noise outside; the screech of a gull, perhaps, or one of those CIE buses putting on its brakes. Then somebody pulls back a curtain and there it is, morning, with the gulls carking round the dustbins, or sitting on top of flag poles, and the ducks quacking off on their sharp morning flight round Stephen's Green. So there is nothing for it but to foot it homeward as best one may.

If I think of myself as the poet O'Bruadair, I think of Nora as Granuaile,[1] the Pirate Queen of the West;[2] she who, being invited

---

[1] Also called Grainne O'Maille or Grace O'Malley. Born about 1530, she was the hereditary chieftain of the O'Malleys. With her first husband, chief of the O'Flahertys, she controlled most of the Western coast including what are now the counties of Mayo, Galway and Clare. Her headquarters were in the Aran Islands and she had another castle and naval base on Clare Island off

to the court of Queen Elizabeth I, took the precaution of bringing two hundred hairy Connacht seamen with her as a bodyguard; a wise move knowing Elizabeth's predilection for throwing potential rivals into the Tower of London. On the voyage over Granuaile gave birth to a son by her second husband Richard 'Iron Dick' Burke. The boy was known as Tibbot na long or Theobald of the Ships and became the first Viscount Mayo.

Gloriana at the time was pursuing a policy of appeasement in Ireland since she had need of her navy for other purposes. To this end she offered Granuaile a barony. The Queen of the West, none the worse for her confinement at sea, replied with the following words: 'I don't want any of your titles. Are we not both equal in the world and would it not be as well for me to make a Countess of you?' It was possibly Queen Elizabeth who remarked, 'She has the mind of a man but the faults of a woman.'

On her way back from England (1594) Granuaile put in with her fleet at Howth to shelter from bad weather. There she sought hospitality from the then Earl of Howth but found instead the gates of the castle barred against her. Infuriated at this churlish behaviour, she kidnapped the Earl's son and heir, a ten-year-old boy, and took him back to the West. Later she returned him on condition that the family should ever after give shelter to all mariners who had need to put into Howth harbour. The terms were accepted and the bargain kept, and to this day an extra place is laid at table for any seafarer who may have occasion to call.

Nora FitzGerald is a latter-day Granuaile, and behind the wheel of her Lagonda some would say she is as dangerous as the Queen was in her war galley. But Nora's puissance is somewhat – though only somewhat – curtailed by the age in which she lives. Had she been born one generation earlier she would I think have been with Pearse and Connolly at the siege of the Post Office or,

---

Westport from where she carried out her 'thrade of maintainance by sea and land'.

[2] 'Grany O'Mayle, a woman that hath impudently past the part of woman-hood, and being a great spoiler, and chief Commander of thieves and murtherers at sea, to spoil this province.' – State Paper Office.

more likely, with her own myrmidons defending the Shelbourne Hotel to the last man, last woman, and last round.

Dudley Walsh, lawyer, literary man, two-fisted drinker, Dubliner *par excellence*, Gogarty's verse to his boon companion describes you well:

> *If medals were ordained for drinks,*
> *Or soft communings with a minx,*
> *Or being at your ease belated,*
> *By Heavens, you'd be decorated,*
> *And not Alcmena's chesty son*[1]
> *Have room to put your ribbands on!*

But why do you keep me out of my bed all and every night? To read to me about 'Cunty Kate' and 'Biddy-the-Clap' in the vernacular? To describe to me how your cousin Walter Starkie fiddled to the gypsies of Andalusia in elastic-sided boots, and had to jump out of window to escape a homicidal *gitano* with a knife? Or is it that you just dare not take the risk of falling into the arms of Lethe? Whatever the reason, rest easy wherever you may now be.

When I go to the West I stop half way with Dudley's friend (and relative by marriage) Desmond Williams and with his wife Brenda, who is Oliver St John Gogarty's only daughter.

Following the River Shannon downstream from Leitrim through Roscommon to Athlone, and then on a few miles to the south, one comes eventually to Clonmacnois – Clonmacnois of the Seven Churches. This is in the very centre of Ireland and it is nearby, at a place called Tullamore, that my friends live.

Brenda, daughter of the man Yeats described as 'one of the great lyric poets of our age', is a sculptor. Her husband, Desmond, is a man of many interests and the ones he and I share in particular are boats and sailing – by which I mean sailing in boats, and wild life in the sense of wild birds and wild-fowl, which last can best be seen while sailing in boats. It is all one syndrome because Tullamore is in the centre of Ireland, and Tullamore is on the road to the West. And Tullamore is near the Shannon and the Shannon

[1] Hercules.

156

leads to the sea. And, if a point could be stretched, Granuaile is part of the syndrome too because she has a castle on Clare Island, and Clare Island is in Clew Bay. And Clew Bay has three hundred and sixty-five islands. And Desmond has a boat called a *pucaun*, gaff-rigged, carvel-built, and only a little bit later in concept than the one used by St Brendan to discover America. And it is in the *pucaun* that we sail round the three hundred and sixty-five islands of Clew Bay to fish for mackerel to bait our hooks to catch ray, bass, pollock, conger, dog-fish, tope[1] and anything else whose fancy we manage to tickle.

And there is always a porpoise close behind you. It could even be Grace O'Malley because the people of the West are frequently transubstantiated into the warm-blooded creatures of the sea. When Louis Le Brocquy was fishing once off the coast of Mayo he looked up from his business of baiting a hook to see a pair of large, brown, beautiful and absolutely human eyes regarding him. The boatman saw it too, and being a local man, addressed the onlooker civilly. 'Hullo, Keneally,' he said. The Keneally, or Conolly family, who are numerous on that coast, tend to return and inhabit the bodies of seals.

Another time on the Great Blasket[2] a young man was out hunting seals when he came into a cave by the water's edge where there was a cow-seal with her young calf. Seeing him the cow-seal spoke out: 'If you are in luck,' she said, 'you will leave this cove in haste, for be it known to you that you will not easily kill my little son.'

One beautiful day with the sun shining, a fresh breeze blowing, and not a cloud in the sky we set sail for Clare and Grainne O'Maille's castle. We took Desmond's paid hand with us, an old fisherman who has lived a long life in constant dread of the sea. When we got out into open water the man tried to put the *pucaun*'s head around and when Desmond asked him why, he said he didn't like the look of the weather. Since it was the best day of the year, Desmond put the question to him again a little more tersely.

'Ah, God,' said the old man, ' 'tis too fine altogether.'

[1] Member of the shark family.
[2] The largest of a group of islands off the coast of Kerry.

We went to Clare Island nevertheless – and came back again, thanks be to God and none to the old sailor.

But I have got to the West too soon. The centre of Ireland has a character all of its own. From the Great Bog of Allen to the Shannon River is low-lying country and the haunt of snipe and lapwing, golden plover and heavy duck, and migratory geese in their season.

The Seven Churches of Clonmacnois stand on rising ground overlooking the flat callows of the Shannon, grey in their melancholy granite, cold as the low skies that blow over them. On the wind which never ceases is the sound of curlew and scall-crow,[1] and plover and peewit, and the sound of the wind itself blowing through thorns and grasses and the holes in the stones.

Many times have I been there to marvel at the work of those ancient holy men who, at the dawn of the Celtic twilight, came down daily from the round and draughty tower to worship God and to execute in His name their monumental sculptures and hieroglyphs.

> The host is riding from Knocknarea
> And over the grave of Clooth-na-Bare;
> Caoilte tossing his burning hair,
> And Niamh calling Away, come away . . .

It would be a cold business to live and to die and to be buried at Clonmacnois. Many times have I shot the callows there, and at Shannonbridge and Banagher too, walking up snipe or waiting crouched in a gripe for the swift flocks of 'goldies' to come whistling down the wind.

At Banagher lives Danny Moran who is not a poacher turned gamekeeper, but one who makes a living in both capacities.

On cold mornings before a shoot the guns rendezvous at a bar there and have a jar or two 'to straighten out the barrels'. On one such morning Danny had had a jar or three and the first thing he did was to shoot a hare stone dead right between the legs of Desmond's brother Vincent. It was the first shot of the morning and Vincent was not so much damaged as shocked. He let out a strong curse at Danny who, still chasing the whiskey round

[1] *Corvus corone cornix.*

his mouth, said, 'Ah, bejasus, I could be shooting gnats this minute.'

The bogs for economic reasons are now being drained and in consequence the native birds that breed there are leaving. Soon there will be no grouse left, but Desmond has shot them in this part of the country for years, and I have sometimes been with him. Danny Moran it is who builds the butts and who arranges for the beaters to drive the birds towards them. When the grouse are flushed a shout goes up and the dark birds, hard to see against the brown bog, come in fast and low down wind. Then for a moment there is pandemonium as they come to the line of guns.

Obviously, when shooting from a butt, the gun can shoot before, behind or above it but, naturally, he cannot fire down the line without peppering his companions. On the day I have in mind, by about the third drive, there was such a hail of lead coming down the butts that nobody was bothering about the grouse at all, only watching out to duck every time the man called Rooney of the Doon pulled the trigger.

Eventually Desmond sauntered over to Rooney to suggest tactfully that he might prefer to fire only at the high birds. When he got there the first thing his sharp eye saw at the bottom of the butt among the empty cartridges was three empty naggins of whiskey. What really put the edge on Desmond's irritation – and I should mention that he is a distiller with a low irascibility point – was that the whiskey was not of his (Desmond's) making.

The story is told that Rooney one day found himself short of money in a part of the country where he was unknown. He went into a bank and presented his cheque book but the cashier declined to give him any money.

'But,' said your man, 'I am Rooney of the Doon.'

'I don't care,' said the cashier, 'if you are Mooney of the Moon. You don't get cash here.'

One evening, at nightfall, tired after a day walking the bog, Desmond and his brother-in-law, Oliver Gogarty, went into the bar at Shannonbridge to warm themselves up before driving home. They went through to the small snug at the back which was quite dark except for the glow coming from an ancient stove. And there they sat with the place to themselves enjoying each

159

other's conversation over their balls of malt. Only after a while did they become aware of a sound that, at more or less regular intervals, emanated from the hot stove. It was the sound of a sharp hiss.

As the whiskey warmed them, so did it enliven their conversation which became spiced with anecdotes of a humorous but slanderous nature. They had been engaged in this innocuous pastime for about an hour before they became aware of something stirring in the darkest corner of the stove. The 'something' was a 'someone' who, rising to his anonymous feet, sent one last gob of spit sizzling on to the stove before walking out with his stolen earful.

If I think of the Shannon in terms of 'Red Hanrahan' and the 'Hostings of the Sidhe', the West I see through the eyes of the poet's brother Jack.

Jack B. Yeats, the painter, is very much a poet too. To know this you only have to look at his pictures called 'The man on the wild one waved his hat', or 'Singing under the canopy of Heaven', or 'Queen Maeve walked upon this Strand'. His blacks and raw blues, high-lighted here and there with white and the purest yellows and reds, have an effect that can only find a parallel in a choice piece of native tweed. I have an old suit that is pure Jack Yeats and I have half a mind to frame it and put it in the hands of the good Victor Waddington, who may have helped to make Jack as famous as his brother.

The brothers Yeats are Sligo men where, under the shadow of Ben Bulben, W.B. now lies buried.

> Cast a cold eye
> On life, on death,
> Horseman, pass by!

From Mayo came Raftery, the poet and balladeer, whose nostalgia for his home county is as catching as the pox, a dose of which he caught at an early age. It blinded the poor fellow for life.

'Now with the coming in of the spring,' Raftery says, 'I shall hoist my flag and go. For since the thought came into my head I can neither stand nor sit until I find myself in the middle of the County of Mayo.'

It was in Mayo, at a place called Killala, that Napoleon, or more accurately the French Directory, landed a small army in the year 1798, at a time when Raftery was still a young boy. 'The Year of the French' is an historical cul-de-sac which, had it succeeded, could have altered the main road of history by giving the Napoleonic forces a spring-board for the invasion of England. Fortunately for the British, Bonaparte's *Fingerspitzengefühl* led him to Egypt instead, and his army in Ireland became a forlorn hope and a forgotten memory, all except to the people of Mayo, God help them.

Blind Raftery was by all accounts an independent man and a convivial personality.

'In Claremorris,' he says, 'I will stop a night and sleep with dacent men, and then go on to Balla just beyond and drink galore. And next to Kiltamagh for a visit of about a month, and then I would only be a couple of miles from Ballinamore.'

Sightless as he was, he went his way round the West of Ireland making a living singing songs and writing verses. He crossed the bogs by himself and if he came to a dyke he would pace his run backwards from its edge and jump it fearlessly. He never sought a quarrel but, in case the edge of his tongue was not quite sharp enough, he carried a wide-bladed knife under his armpit and was said to have used it on occasion. He was a well-respected man.

Oliver St John Gogarty, the wit and ear, nose and throat specialist, once wrote:

> *It is not everyone gets on*
> *Where dwell the Seaside sons of Conn:*
> *It is not everyone that's wanted*
> *Where things are apt to be enchanted.*

Gogarty is to Galway as Joyce is to Dublin, bard and chronicler in contemporary idiom, and it is through him more than any other poet or writer that this old pile comes alive – Galway, an archipelago in grey granite leaning into the westerly wind and the Atlantic. Only the Aran Islands and that Celtic lost Atlantis, legendary Hy-Brasil, comes between her and the New World.

Ᵹᴀɪʟʟⁱᵐ (pronounced Goll-yiv), the City of Galway, is the capital of Connacht and was the ancient seaport of the Western

World at a time when Bristol and Liverpool were scarcely heard of outside Britain. Today the docks, granaries and warehouses, superbly built in monumental slabs of granite, stand indestructible, grown with weed, idle and beautiful, silent but not forlorn. By the dockside squats the Spanish Arch, a wind-bent thorn tree growing out of its roof, and beside it, strangely juxtaposed, a sub-tropical palm. On the same roof, beneath the trees, stands Clare Sheridan's 'Madonna and Child' carved from an older and thicker thorn. Below, Corrib pours its salmon torrent over the old stones below the Arch and into the harbour where the skeletons of old hulks lie like flenched whales. Around them swans in their hundreds, silent and serious, propel themselves about their mysterious business, and gulls wheel and cry over the restless water.

Galway, once a quasi-independent mercantile city-republic, is known as the City of the Tribes: fourteen families of Anglo-Norman settlers named variously Athy, Kirwan, Lynch, Blake, Bodkin, Browne, Deane,[1] Ffrench, Font, Martin, Joyce, Skerret, Morris and D'Arcy – and many good Irishmen living today, not only in Galway, bear those names. These families built up the city and the seaport in the thirteenth and fourteenth centuries and pushed the Burkes and the native Irish into Connemara and Mayo where Gaeltachts, or Irish-speaking communities, still exist.

In 1493 the Mayor of Galway was one James Lynch[2] who found himself in his official capacity obliged to try his own son for the murder of a Spanish friend. (The story goes they had quarrelled over a girl.) Guilt was admitted and, despite strong pleas for clemency from all sides, Lynch – so above nepotism was he – duly passed sentence of death by hanging. But the story does not end there. The citizens, roused to sympathy for the son and his mother, demonstrated against the execution and intimidated the hangman. Notwithstanding, the father, determined to see justice done, slipped a noose around the boy's neck and 'launched him into Eternity' with his own hand. The window where the deed was done is still to be seen. Descendants of the same family subse-

[1] A name given to my brother Michael, after our maternal grandmother, née Maude Deane.
[2] The Lynch who gave his name to 'Lynch law' was an American.

quently came to own Château Lynch-Bages in Bordeaux, whose wine is popular in Galway today.

A story is told of the present Bishop of Galway, Dr Browne (another 'tribesman'), who recently issued an edict that no priest in his diocese was to be seen smoking in public. One day, motoring in the country, he saw a priest sitting on a bridge watching the salmon rise as he smoked his pipe. Angry at being thus flouted he stopped the car and sent his chaplain to remonstrate. 'Excuse me, Father,' said the chaplain, 'but you know that the Bishop of Galway does not allow the clergy to smoke in public.'

'Tell the Bishop of Galway,' said the offending priest in a strong American accent, 'that the Bishop of Baltimore smokes his pipe when and where he pleases.'

Clare Sheridan, sculptor, painter, writer, traveller, and at various times the intimate friend of Lenin, Mussolini, Primo de Rivera, *int al*, was herself related to an American Indian Chief. She lived at one time in Oranmore Castle, a massive Norman keep, standing on the rocky butt of the bay of Galway looking westward over basking seals and swirling seaweed toward Black Head and the Aran Islands. Here by the water's edge are huge black rocks mottled in white and saffron lichens, and on to them oyster-catchers drop molluscs to split them open. Nearby in the sparse and salty fields scall-crows peck at the eyes of dead sheep or investigate the guts of rabbits. Here and there about the castle are granite monoliths still showing the signs of the sculptor's chisel but which now, in the abandonment of time, are growing back into the landscape as moss and lichen, nettles and ivy, gradually reclaim them.

One day I went to the castle to see a man I know called Peter Wilson who was living there. Before going into the house I walked down to the water's edge and there I saw a girl with strawberry hair. At that moment in time I think she was the most beautiful girl I had ever seen. Through the seaweed undulating in the little waves she was riding a grey horse, astride in an Arab saddle with red woollen tassels hanging almost to the water. Although I now forget everything else about the girl – her name, where she came from, where she was going – I shall never forget the sight of her that day with her red hair and red saddle on the grey horse against the grey sea and the grey Galway sky over her head. It was of course Niamh, daughter of Aengus and Edain, whom Oisin found 'on the dove-grey edge of the sea', and I, like Oisin, was bewitched – but, mercifully, for less than an hundred years.

14

There has never been a time in my life since I was about thirteen years old when I have not been in love. My affair with Cathleen, the daughter of Houlihan, has in one sense been a typically Irish one insofar as it has been going on a very long time. It has on the other hand also been a permissive one in that I have been able at the same time to pay court to a young lady in Dublin who very properly, and very nicely, turned me down since, of course, I am not eligible. But this too has been happy and instructive because there is no better way of learning about a country, its people, and its language[1] than by being in love with one of its citizens.

Also part of this attachment is my infatuation with the strawberry-headed girl in Galway, but she is more in the nature of a myth, the negative of the positive of An Roisin Dubh – dark Rosaleen – whom I have never actually met.

Inspired by this multiplex affair, therefore, I have made some study of Irish literature, Irish history, and the Catholic faith. I have long been a Roman Catholic by prejudice and I have now gone some way to becoming an Irish Nationalist by conviction. Well, everybody is influenced by the person with whom they are in love.

It is eight years since the war ended and nearly thirteen since I put brush to canvas. I was sitting in a London pub the other day when I saw a woman with magenta cheeks, white double-chins and a black bombazine bosom with a rose in it, and suddenly I wanted to paint her more than anything in the world. I felt a blush rising up from my stomach, flushing up my carotid artery and doubling the intensity of my normally red face. I was completely taken by surprise and was, you might say, overwhelmed by the strength of my emotion. I must, I felt, start to paint again at all cost, but where, when, and with what? Then the thought of the sheer impossibility of my finances and general predicament made

[1] This is not meant to imply that I have learned Gaelic.

the blood drain down out of my cheeks again, to drip back disconsolately into my heart.

Of course there is always writing. I wrote my first book when I was nine, a crib of G. A. Henty with a bit of Kipling thrown in: thirteen pages complete with illustrations. I have done less well since. Cyril Connolly was going to publish some war stuff of mine in *Horizon*. This was in 1944, 'invasion' time, and I never delivered the final MS. Later I did a war book and offered it to Nicholson and Watson, but they said that everybody was sick of the war and they didn't want to publish. I wrote another and offered it to Batsford who said it was beautifully written but 'nothing happens'. Some years later I wrote a revised version cannibalizing both books and offered it to Nicholson and Watson again. This time they said that they had published so many war books the public was sick of them.

More recently I have been writing a few short stories and have passed some on to Maurice Richardson, the writer and critic. He passed them on to some editor friend of his who said they were fine 'as exercises', but that their influences were too obvious. So help me God, I wasn't aware of any influences when I wrote them. But I suppose, thinking back, Joyce and Hemingway must have been there respectively breathing Power's Gold Label and Valpolicella down my neck.

All the same, Maurice has been very encouraging. He says that most people who start to write should have their pens broken in public at the outset. But, he says, if he were the judge he would allow me to keep my pen intact.

But now I have got to do something. What?

*   *   *

Scratch, scratch. Squeak, squeak, squeak. Tap, tap, tap, tap. Lettice is upstairs in bed and I am sitting under a lamp scratching with a diamond-point on an old rummer.

It all started one evening in the country when I came across some photographs of engraved glass by Laurence Whistler. Though mid-winter, it was a fine night and I went out of doors before going to bed. There was a frost and when I looked up at the sky I saw the man-in-the-moon as clearly as anything; so much so that I had the conceit of being able to lip-read what he was trying to say. But I was not really interested in that. What I have always been interested in is portraiture, and here was the most obvious model for a portrait on glass in the very medium of light itself. And so the first engraving on glass I ever did was a portrait of the man-in-the-moon.

And suddenly I saw everything in the winter landscape of England translated into the refraction of light: mist floating in the valley bottom, rime lying in the shadows, the yew and the monkey-puzzle black against the hoarfrost, wisps of straw on a dead hedgerow, black ivy like a dancer's wig keeping the draught off a tree stump: blackthorn draped with old-man's-beard, the sharp ridges of plough, the ice in the furrow, the tines on the harrow, the steaming midden, the drop on the end of an old man's nose, Robert-at-the-door, and Jenkins-in-the-soup. Tap, tap, tap. Squeak, squeak. Scratch, scratch, scratch.

After a bit I get sleepy, and cross over to an armchair. Over my pyjamas I am wearing my poshteen – otherwise known as a Hebron coat, a rough ankle-length sheepskin which the Palestinian shepherds wear in winter. I have had it ever since the war in the Western Desert and if it is now a bit smelly, it is also very warm and comforting. No doubt I fell asleep quite quickly because the next thing I remember is being woken in panic by the sensation of a live creature wriggling next to my skin. I jump to my feet in horror and start leaping about the room, hysterically beating at my body as if in a nightmare. But it is no dream. From the area of my stomach issues *mus domesticus*, the common mouse. It skids down my trouser leg half-stunned, and totters off towards its hole in the corner. Attracted I suppose by the smell and the warmth, it had climbed up inside my trousers as I slept. I ask you! What the hell next?

Engraving is, I suppose, some release for the night-time hours, as are bibulous lunches with my wine trade pals during the day. There is one other.

Dugald MacFie lives in a sea-going Thames barge moored upstream of the Tate Gallery alongside a place called Dolphin Square. Dugald is a professional soldier who speaks Russian and who has some mysterious job in the War Office. I suspect it is putting microphones in visiting diplomats' bedrooms. I don't know. He never lets on, of course, but he is very keen on electronics and is always playing about with tape-recorders and things.

The barge, which used to belong to Peter Wilson (the same man who is now living in Oranmore Castle) is called *Harold*. She has been well, but not luxuriously, converted and what was formerly the hold makes a wide and comfortable saloon amidships. There is also an after-cabin for the crew which has one bunk lying athwartships right in the stern. This is a lovely place to lie and to drift off to sleep feeling the lift of the tide beneath one and the slap of water on the hull.

There are many things that make sailing in a Thames barge different to any other. In the first place all gear is extremely heavy and most of it has to be moved by manpowered winch. This includes the enormous piece of timber called a sprit from which the mainsail is hoist. There are also heavy wooden lee-boards, one either side, which are lowered to prevent the flat-bottomed hull from making too much leeway. The great red sails themselves, which look so graceful at a distance, are made from canvas hard as iron and dressed with a mixture of ochre and fish-glue. The first day's sailing is usually, therefore, a chronicle of aching stomach muscles, blistered hands, broken knuckles, bent finger nails, and nausea induced by the stink of rotting fish.

For all that, *Harold*, skippered by Dugald, handles beautifully and once out in the open sea has an easy motion and a surprising turn of speed; or perhaps not so surprising when one considers the vast area of reeking, fish-daubed canvas aloft. But for me the most enjoyable thing about a barge is the sensation one has of sailing not in a boat, nor in a yacht, but in a ship.

There is only one snag about *Harold* and that is her cabin-boy, O'Malley. She is a young woman formerly married to one of the O'Malley's of Westport (kinsmen of Granuaile), and I have, of course, fallen in love with her.

The barge's sailing schedule, owing to the shore-going occupation of her master, is restricted to weekends or to such time as Dugald and his crew can take off. But there is pleasure and adventure to be had in the Thames estuary and in coastal waters, whether it is sailing north to Brightlingsea or south to the Nore and the Cinque Ports. And no small part of the joy of this vessel is that she has a big galley, an effective stove, a good sea-cook in Rhona O'Malley, and a more than adequate commissariat.

A Thames barge in the open sea is an inspiring sight with her giant sprit and huge areas of ochre canvas, and to be at the wheel under full sail is an exhilarating experience.

We are so sailing one day about six miles off the Essex Coast in a fresh breeze near Buxey Sands. Rhona below, Dugald doing something up forward and myself at the wheel, thoroughly content, with one eye on the compass and the other (so to speak) on the sails aloft. Suddenly, although there is no sound, no change in the wind, no overt sign of anything strange at all, *Harold* ceases to answer the helm. The sails are full, the sea is running, the wheel spins freely in my hands. Then nothing. We have ceased to move. We have become ghost people in a phantom ship. I let out a yell to Dugald but it disappears into the shrouds like the cry of some strange seabird on shadowy waters.

But he has seen what has happened. Quite simply the out-going tide has imperceptibly lowered our flat-bottomed craft on to hard sand which could not be seen for the churned up water. We quickly lower sail – that is to say as quickly as possible considering the length of time it takes to lower those huge areas of fish-glued, salt-sprayed, bone-hard canvas. Within half an hour we are high and dry and able to walk overboard – I cannot say ashore because we are out of sight of land. It is a strange and solitary thing to be with a stranded ship on a summer afternoon on an off-shore island of sand alone among the molluscs and starfish and the distant pale waves.

In course of time the tide lifts us again as gently as it set us down. The sails slowly heave us into motion and off we go once more over the shallow pea-green sea.

And so at the grey end of the day we round West Swin whose solemn bell-buoy in flat tones tolls the coming of night, clang-clanging its bell alone at the ebb and slop of barnacled hull, seemingly for all the world without end.

Will I ever get out of this? Will I ever break out again? *Harold* is a brief solace, Ireland is a chimera, Rhona O'Malley is an ache of yearning and I am in a dark dungeon of my own making, in a state of black despair.

We have moved into a larger and gloomier flat. It is a wet October afternoon and I am staring out of the window at a vista of Queens Gate Gardens in the rain.

Lettice has gone out and as usual has left the wireless on and I, for once, have not switched it off. It now begins to play Dvorak's 'cello concerto and the sad sounds of the solo instrument begin to merge with, and finally engulf, my own sadness. Soon I am able to transfer my unhappiness to the 'cello itself and this becomes an easement of the pain. But when the music stops my misery comes flooding back again.

Oh God, I have never turned to You in the hour of danger, in the moment of fear when my life has been in Your hands. Please take this into consideration and give me some comfort now if You will.

Last night Lettice and I had a drunken row. We woke little Harry who came padding out of the nursery in his pyjamas. Later I lay awake thinking of what we had done to him. Of how much is he aware, I wonder? Has some traumatic shock been inflicted on him? Has deep and irreparable damage been done? This morning he went off to school happily practising his new grin.

The concerto over, despairingly I go out into the wet street. The first human being I see is a thin middle-aged negro, an African surely, for he is wearing knickerbockers, puttees, a double-breasted blue jacket, a white stock, and a cap with a bobble on top. What can have brought him to this sunless desert, poor bastard.

Further on a young man, lesser public school and business suited, looks pleased with himself with a palpably new hat and new umbrella. As confident as the African is apprehensive, he seems every bit as hopeless and my heart bleeds for him, too.

Yet further, I catch a glimpse of Babette, a gentle Jewess I used to know at art school. She has gone a bit grey and she is thinner, but her eyes are even larger and softer than before. A wedding ring? Perhaps – I couldn't really see. I hope you are happy, Babette.

At the bar is a thin grey woman on the last of her sparrow's legs.

She invests in a small glass of gin and, having paid the exact sum in small change, she bears it away to a table, walking with slow stiff movements like a heron with a fish in its beak. She sits upright on the edge of the seat and sips at the spirits, her eyes unseeing, looking straight ahead of her. She takes little sups holding the glass by the stem, little finger extended, feeling the warmth of the liquor entering her old cold frame.

When one is truly unhappy one shares the sorrows of the world and everyman's misfortune is one's own. Today I feel compassion for everybody I see, for the lonely negro in the knickerbockers, for the complacent young man in his hopeless outfit, for the gentle Babette, for the old lady buying her tot of life-giving gin, for my two children, small and dear, and for my wife.

Il pleut dans mon coeur,
Comme il pleut sur la ville

– and it never rains but it pours.

15

'Did you hear about that poor old bloke what was on holiday with his wife and kids at the seaside?' says the old tot who is supposed to muck me out. 'Only went into the urinal for a slash and they done for him. Bashed his head right in. Brains all over the floor. My friend's friend who's a cleaner says she never saw such a . . .'

'There is nothing about it in the paper,' I say, hoping to shut her up.

'Yes, well,' she goes on, 'this old girl says when she done clearing up there was a whole bucket full of . . .'

Morning does not become Clara. In the first place she gets up at five to go to the House of Commons. By the time she gets back to me in Battersea, where she started out from, she is badly in need of a pick-me-up and usually helps herself to a large port and Worcestershire sauce if I have got any. Having downed this she is not only willing, but anxious, to dish up the rest of the over-night gossip which she has either experienced personally, or gleaned from the other old girls as they muck out the Mother of Parliaments.

The great palace would be shamed, if we at
daybreak failed to come with sweeping brushes.
We clean away, each time, a night's offences,
lest the dawn complain.[1]

'As I was going home last night, this bloke came out of a telephone box flashing off his winkle. "Mind you don't get it frost bit, my lad," I said. . . .'

There is always something. Yesterday the strong wind blew an old age pensioner under a bus. The day before two more dangerous prisoners escaped from the Scrubs. As a matutinal stimulant Clara is better than a dose of salts.

Today the sun is shining and it has ceased to be so cold. And

[1] Josep Carner, trans. Pearse Hutchinson.

suddenly I am overwhelmed by the feeling that life – the thing itself, not the events in it – is so superb, so ravishing. No longer am I Sisyphus forever pushing a boulder uphill. Today I feel like Icarus at take-off, like a satyr in a glade of Naiads, an aubade singer in the Elysian fields, a whistler in the eye of the wind, a rider to the sea. In fact, this morning, I feel like Reilly on the pig's back.

I do not want to go into detail about leaving Lettice and the children. It is too painful and too recent. It is enough to say that I left and, having left, went to the Cavendish Hotel in Jermyn Street where I asked for the cheapest room in the house. Edith, Rosa Lewis's niece, compromised by letting me have a top room at the back for a peppercorn rate provided I would render occasional assistance to the one-legged Major who lives on the same floor. I did not realize at the time that the Major came back drunk every night of his life. For a disciplinary exercise, I can recommend trying to get into a tiny lift and out again, into a lavatory and out again, and finally into bed and sometimes out again, a drunk who cannot stand up on two legs, let alone one. It would be enough to make St Vincent de Paul swear. But it was worth the penance because everybody was so kind to me at the Cavendish and one needs the home-from-home comforts in situations such as mine.

Then life, having changed so radically, started to change again with such rapidity that I found myself laughing for the first time since my departure from the aforesaid matrimonial home.

First I ran into Louis Le Brocquy whom I had known slightly in Ireland. Certain people, as I have tried to demonstrate, have at various times changed the whole course of my life. Louis now joined their number. 'There is a studio going a few doors down from me,' he said. 'Quite cheap. Would you like it?'

So life began anew at 6, Albert Studios. Eight in number, these William Morris-ish studios lie in a tree-locked enclave in the hinterland south of the Albert Bridge. Concealed in a narrow re-entrant among tall aspens and bits of abstract sculpture, they remain, even in winter, half-hidden by evergreens and last year's dead leaves. This muses bower, this elfin grot must have been some cross-fertilization between a wishful dream of mine and some filmic concept of Jean Cocteau that, wafting about in the ether out of space and out of time, had met and spawned – a place. So it was for me; no Underworld but Arcady.

I ran into Clara in a pub when I first came to live in Battersea. This diminutive old string bag whose calves couldn't fill her stockings, who had a hank of tobacco-stained hair half concealing a nasty-looking scar on her head (where she had fallen down drunk at Southend, it transpired), squeezed her way through to the bar next to me and, banging on the counter with a half-crown, ordered 'Ten Woodbines, a strip of Aspro and a Mackeson'. So nauseated was I by the nature of her purchase, conjuring up as it did an aeon of hangovers, that I ordered her a gin. She lowered it in one and chased it with the stout. She then shook me by the hand, leant her elbow in a puddle of beer on the bar, and stood another round. Thus did our relationship become established. She has been a part of my establishment ever since.

When I arrived at Albert Studios Louis himself had not long been in residence. Previously he had shared an extraordinary ménage in another part of London with three other men, one of whom was Declan Papadopoulos. Declan had invented a muska-teerish credo for the household which was simply 'All for one, and that one Declan' – except of course when the duns called, which they did at intervals. Then he passed by any other name. Louis, whose ignorance of these pseudonyms gave some plausi-bility to his blank expression on these occasions, only began to connect the one with the other when he heard Declan snarling and spitting as he took flight out of a back window doing up his flies in mid-air. But after a while the high – and not infrequently low – jinks that took place in that establishment began to interfere too much with Louis's work so that he sought a place of his own elsewhere.

And so gradually a way of life started to impose itself on the two of us. Respecting absolutely our individual privacies, we nevertheless found ways of improving our state of bachelordom. For example, if neither of us had other plans, we would share the burden of commissariat by the pleasant fashion of messing to-gether, taking it in turn to cook. This led to the practice of entertaining jointly when, in time, we began to have more and more friends in common. The system did not of course apply if the entertainment was of an intimate nature; nor did we ever under any circumstances call on each other unheralded, though we lived only two doors apart. Communication without intrusion was effected by the use of a field-telephone kindly provided by the amiable Dugald MacFie.

Time passes and time hovers o'er. Girls come, and stay awhile, and go. The painter Le Brocquy works away and I watch. Apart from the usual sorts of pigment, he uses wax and inks and sand and bits of rag and wool. He also makes tapestries woven to his design at Aubusson, but mostly his work is in oil on canvas and whenever I am free I sit with him and observe. Painting thus, vicariously, I am for that little while freed from my own lust to start where I left off in Montparnasse – how long ago? Fifteen years?

But this morning, as I say, is so clean, so bright, so perfect that I don't in the least mind having to try to sell some Sparkling Red Burgundy to a hard case in Southwark. If I start early enough, I'll be able to have a look at the Italian Exhibition on the way.

I arrived at the New Burlington Gallery just as it opened: paintings mainly abstract, lovely bronzes, some huge smooth forms in white plaster, Emilio Greco's colossal head in terracotta ten times life size, the whole place full of light, colour and exuberance.

As the gallery started to fill up with its morning clientele of the silent and the studious, I began to sense one presence out of concert with the rest. I turned to see a small dandified old man, bouncing up and down on the balls of his feet, grinning angrily at one of the exhibits. My turning to look was a mistake. The little man caught my eye and in a loud high voice called out, 'Ever seen a leg that looked like that?'

The whole room froze; then all turned to look, not at the little man, but at me. Overcome with embarrassment, and being unprepared, unwilling, as well as unqualified to give a lecture on abstract art, I murmured some inaudible negative. The little man then turned triumphantly to the rest of the gallery (who by this time were looking assiduously at the exhibits again) and shouted in an even bigger voice: 'Nor have I, and I've been knocking about the world for eighty years.' Then grinning maliciously, he marched in triumph out of the gallery.

Later I walked slowly over London Bridge in the sunlight looking down at the muddy river bearing its flotsam of orange-peel and old French letters past the Custom House. And I looked across at Hay's wharf and saw the masts of the merchantmen and the cranes and the lighters and the dockyard maties discharging their cargoes. Nearer I looked down at the dirty eddies of turds, timber and old orange-boxes, and the gulls fighting over the jetsam.

Seeing the foreign shipping made me long to be at sea again, to be passing through the Straits of Gibraltar into the Mediterranean, to see the dolphins leaping in and out of the bow-wave, to smell teak decks and hot varnish, to see the sun dancing through the salty porthole on to the bulkhead, to hear the hiss of the sea against the side of the ship.

I walked on through Billingsgate up Fish Street Hill, down Eastcheap, up Mark Lane, passed St Olave's Hart Street, through Crutchéd Friars until I came to my office. Time, if only there was a little more time.

As I passed the trap-doors of our cellars, I gave the conventional shout of 'Bee-low', and back came a cheerful Cockney shout of 'Ull-ow'. I went below and drank a glass of wine with the cellarmen.

> On the banks of the Ban, sure,
> When first I beheld her
> She appeared like young Juno
> The great Grecian queen.
> Her eyes shone like diamonds
> Or stars brightly gleaming;
> Her cheeks bloomed like roses
> Or blood drops on snow.

Louis, Declan and I on occasion sing this song in unison along with a number of other Irish ballads. But whatever it may be like on the banks of the Ban, Albert Studios is pretty good in early summer when the clean new leaves of the poplars hide us in a shimmering screen from the rest of the world, and the giant hollyhocks prevent me from getting in at my door.

As the nights get warmer so does our festive season begin and so do friends make the transpontine trip south to see us. Among our more frequent visitors are the Bomfords from Wiltshire, the O'Connors from Dublin, the Slatterys from Tralee, the Buenos from Madrid and the Beauclerks from Oakley Street just the other side of Albert Bridge. And of course we invite as many attractive girls as we can lay our hands on. Often our entertainments go on into the early morning until, as sometimes happens, the dancing and the singing and the clowning and the charades is interrupted by the arrival of slippered and dressing-gowned figures in pairs furtively scouting through the boskage, ordered out by their wives from the mansions opposite to protest against our noise.

Unpardonably antisocial as is this disturbance of the peace, our parties have never been of a more vicious nature than that engendered by a little drunkenness and the odd flash of lust. There have been no gross debauches, no fights, no daisy-chains, and nothing has ever been smoked more intoxicating than a Gaulloise Bleu.

There have been incidents of course, as for example when Louis and I were misguided enough to bring Nora FitzGerald and Marika Rivera together under the same roof (his). Marika, daughter of the Mexican painter Primo Rivera by a Russian lady known as Marevna, is a dancer and a highly extrovert character – as extrovert as Nora if such a thing were possible.

On the evening that Tunis fell to the 7th Armoured Division in May 1943, from somewhere in the town a female singer with a broken English accent was belting out 'Land of Hope and Glory'. It came in hot, throbbing waves over every public loud-speaker in that oriental city and sounded as appropriate as a Muslim prayer on the Queen's Birthday Parade. It was, as I later found out, Marika. But that was long ago. At this time of the confrontation between herself and Nora bloodshed was happily avoided. Not so subsequently, when a certain young lady, a most agreeable and attractive person under normal circumstances, decided to commit a *crime passionelle*. I was the chosen victim.

The first two frontal attacks were easily thwarted and the lovely girl was variously disarmed of cutlery and other weapons including my carbine, and I only had to have four or five stitches in my hand. She then decided to bide her time.

I should explain that in the studios, all of which are identical, the bedroom is in the gallery, and in the gallery is a skylight, and under the skylight is, of necessity because of the shape of the room, the bed. Her plan, as Louis subsequently discovered, was to climb on to the roof with a boulder and drop it on me in bed through the skylight. She hoped, I think, to pull off the double event by catching me in it with some rival, real or imagined, thus killing two birds, so to speak, with one stone.

This would-be assassin had the strength-to-body ratio of an ant, and from somewhere on Chelsea Embankment where the Council were carrying out some roadworks, she found an enormous jagged slab of concrete which she somehow managed to balance between the handle-bars and seat of her bicycle. With this murderous cargo she was over the hump of Albert Bridge, and was about to freewheel down towards the studios, when she was intercepted by Louis and Jerry Slattery. These two, driving by at a fortunate moment, divined her intention and disarmed her once more. Jerry, being a physician, then administered a strong sedative and Louis, being a philosopher, delivered a soporific lecture on the evil of taking human life. Thereafter, no more attempts were made on mine, though for some time I took good care to make sure who my caller was before opening the door.

The carbine mentioned above had become my 'personal' weapon during the last year of the war. A coloured American somewhere in France had traded it in for a captured Luger automatic and, so strong is the self-preservational habit of infantrymen, I had never again felt safe without it, despite the fact that it had become illegal to retain fire-arms after the war.

Louis, unlike many Irishmen, had never taken part in the war against the Axis, not because he approved of Fascism, nor because he had defective (in the military sense) eyesight, but because he was a convinced pacifist.

One day he came into my studio and was upset to find me oiling up the carbine. In the most forbearing tones he read me a lecture about the obscenity of lethal weapons, making the point that those who possess fire-arms must *ipso facto* wish to use them. In reply I merely said that my possession of the carbine was a romantic habit which, if it had any meaning at all, was associated in my mind with self-defence. Louis persisted with perfect logicality along the lines that, if a gun, why not an atom bomb, and so on.

I began to get bored with Louis's argument at a point when I was wiping the loaded magazine with an oily rag. I gave in to a childish temptation. Quite casually I clipped on the magazine, released the safety-catch, and fired three rounds into an empty orange-box at the other end of the room. The noise was shattering in the confined space and Louis looked stunned. When he had got over his shock he said, 'Don't you see? This just goes to prove my point. I know those were only blanks you were firing but, as I said, if you have a weapon you will one day want to use it with proper bullets.'

'Blanks, Louis?' I said. 'Just come over here.'

We crossed the room and I pointed out three small black holes on the front of the orange-box, and three jagged tears at the back where the bullets had gone right through. I don't think Louis spoke another word for days.

* * *

'You wouldn't catch me coming down here after dark.' said Clara one day. 'I'd be scared of being done in.'

I told her she was a silly old cunt because, although the studios were in a darkish cul-de-sac, the place had always seemed to have the friendliest atmosphere. However, a murder really was committed here one day – in the bushes five yards from Louis's door.

Louis was abroad at the time and his place was shut up. I too was away, and just as well. It happened that a Chelsea doctor whom we both knew very slightly because he did some *locum tenens* work in the neighbourhood, received a sick-call late at night. It was an urgent request to go at once to 3, Albert Studios, this being Louis's address.

No one knows who asked him to be at this rendezvous, or

who met him when he got there. If they do, they know who the murderer is.

The milkman found the body next morning lying among the evergreens. He had been stabbed to death. Louis and I, among many others, were questioned by the police, but we were quite unable, for obvious reasons, to 'help them with their inquiries'.

*   *   *

Apart from that one act of murder and a little mayhem, these last few years have been a time of the greatest domestic felicity. In fact it has been one of the happiest times of my life. However, time, being relative, may go forwards, backwards or sideways but, as most scientists agree, it does not stand still. One can only help it along or leave it alone. Louis and I, out of sheer caprice one day, decided on the former course. The intention was to have a great stirabout in our social lives with an emphasis on the opposite (to us) sex. What was required, in Corporal's Mess terminology, was a sort of 'Gentleman's Spot Excuse-me'. The method was to give a joint party, each one of us inviting all and every attractive female that we had ever met. The venue chosen was my studio.

The day was duly appointed and the guests duly came but, like other capricious schemes, it had side-effects that the schemers had never dreamed of. Louis soon had his glasses on, and his address book out, and was going round the room like a dealer at an auction. The women were certainly a stunning collation and there is no better recipe for a good party than plenty of pretty girls. One of Louis's invitees was a very handsome woman called Frederika Maxwell who ran an art gallery. My prize exhibit, whom I had recently met at the house of some Spanish friends, was a beautiful and vivacious Anglo-Irish painter who looked like a young Virginia Woolf. Her name was Anne Madden-Simpson.

Next day we compared notes. 'What about that girl, Anne – the Irish one with the long fair hair?' I said. 'I thought of asking her round again.'

'You're too late, old chap,' said Louis with a wolfish grin. And so I was. Louis and Anne were married some months later in Chartres Cathedral and I was the best man. At the same time, and almost by osmosis, I found Frederika Maxwell in my life. Finally, though it was no direct consequence of this party, I lost my job. What happened was this. The wine trade, like any other business, has good and bad years. My firm had just had rather a bad one. In addition, though not necessarily due to my lack of industry, my sales figures were down, though my expenses (rising cost of living?) were up. The managing director asked me to take a cut in salary. I refused. We had a nasty little scene in the boardroom and that was that.

*　　*　　*

So here I am, a not-so-young man without a job lying full length on a bunk in front of a stove. It is early afternoon at Winter Solstice with the blackbird in the garden making its nightfall noises as the four o'clock darkness descends on London and on me.

PART THREE

16

So the prospect before us is not exactly promising. Nearly forty years old now and what have I achieved? A trail of broken contracts, an odd short story not badly done, the occasional engraving on glass quite well executed, some split-second moments of vision when the meaning of life in all its beauty seems to have been revealed to me, and nothing – absolutely nothing – else. I ask myself seriously sometimes if Divine Providence did not make a *faux pas* by sparing my life in the war when many better men lost theirs. And then I realize that the grand scheme of things is so grand that this sort of oversight is of no importance at all. And yet . . . and yet – if only I could be struck by a blinding light, a great flash of comprehension such as was given to Paul on the road to Damascus. But then . . . but then – could it be significant that I still have this hope, this belief, this certainty almost, that something is to become of me yet; that sooner or later I shall have a chance to put to some use those small but virulent germs of talent that were given me at birth? Sooner or later? My life is half over. Soon it will be too late.

'But while to propose to be a better man is a piece of unscientific cant, to have become a deeper man is the privilege of those who have suffered.'

The question is, have I suffered enough? Certainly not as much as Oscar Wilde when he wrote *De Profundis* in prison? Who is to say? In any case all is relative, and if I now have reached the winter solstice of my life, it is as certain to change as it is certain that the sun, stationary at its tropic, will move again towards the equator. Will it change for the better, though? Who can say?

Today is my day for collecting the National Assistance handout, or, as it used to be called in less pretentious days, the dole. The Battersea Labour Exchange is just south of the park and it is a pleasant enough walk round the edge of the lake, to watch for a moment the ducks and to cast a fond eye over the Henry Moores. The only trouble is that the man who hands out the cash is a former NCO in the Rifle Brigade and, since I know his face, he must surely know mine, or at least my name which he has inscribed in his ledger. At one time he would have called me 'sir'. Now I feel I ought to say 'sir' to him. Well it is nothing at all to put up with when one thinks of the humiliations suffered by poor Oscar. And anyway this man is as content as I am to keep up the pretence of anonymity. The worse moments of this demeaning condition of being totally without money have been when I have had to make excuses to people like Desmond and other friends from other countries and other days. When they come to London, my lack of hospitality must seem like an affront.

*   *   *

Life, my life, almost everybody's lives seem to be built along a ladder of epiphanies. I have tried here to log mine in such a way as to show how it has, for the most part, been made up of encounters with individuals or groups of people who have altered the direction of my life.

Five years after moving into Albert Studios alongside Louis Le Brocquy, I met a man called Sydney Newman, a Canadian of Russian-Jewish origin, who had just arrived a newcomer to England with a brief to reorganize the drama department of one of the independent television companies.

It happened like this. Michael, my brother, had made friends with a Californian screenwriter called Gustave Field. Gustave had been recruited as dramaturge or story editor by Newman to help him to reconstitute the company's dramatic output. Gustave and his beautiful wife, Daphne, at this time pregnant, were looking for somewhere to live. Louis and Anne Le Brocquy, having married, had now disappeared to Provence. The Fields, therefore, moved into 3, Albert Studios and we there became friends. At some period shortly afterwards I showed Gustave a few of my short stories. One of them he passed on with a recommendation to Sydney Newman who read it and said it would make a good television play. It did. It was called *Small Fish are Sweet*, starring Donald Pleasence and Katherine Blake. It was both a box-office and a critical success. I was only paid £300 for it, but I was from that moment launched upon a new career.

At the time of writing *Small Fish* I was introduced to Newman by Gustave whose motives for effecting the introduction were twofold: first he was sympathetic to the condition of a writer in need of work, and secondly he was so over-worked himself, being inundated with unsolicited scripts, any one of which might have been the work of some great new talent,[1] that he was badly in need of an assistant.

The meeting with Newman was, of course, another epiphany. It was even epoch-making in a minor way. At first impact I had never met anybody so 'American' in my life, and apparently he had never met anybody quite so 'English', which simply proves, if proof were needed, that environment makyth man. And so began a series of contemporary British plays known as 'Armchair Theatre'. It is true that the title had already come into being under the suzerainty of Dennis Vance who had put out a miscellany of revivals and adaptations of stage plays. But the era of contemporary plays by new writers only came into being under the *imprimatur* and *nihil obstat* of Sydney Newman. It was a new wave, and it rose and fell in the kitchen sink.

Nor were the three of us, Sydney, Gustave and myself, the only people to put the wind behind it, but to chronicle all concerned would be irrelevant here, there were so many. Even old pal Papadopoulos briefly had a grubby finger in the pie. After a short while though, he was caught playing ducks-and-drakes with his expense account (one item at the end of a long bill was £4 for entertaining Arthur Koestler to brandy), and he left.

The terms of my own employment were far from satisfactory. Despite the fact that I was desperate for a job in order to meet my family commitments, I nevertheless clung with equal desperation to my new freedom – or what I could of it. In the end I was signed on by Sydney Newman as Assistant Story Editor at the rate of just over £1,000 a year to work a five-day week; the other two days being free for my own work. What in fact happened was that I found myself working seven days a week, sixteen hours a day for Sydney Newman, and any time for my own writing had to be found out of the eight hours allocated to sleep.

[1] In fact at least two of them were: *The Dumb Waiter* by Harold Pinter and *Progress to the Park* by Alun Owen.

Well I couldn't, and didn't, complain. At least not for a long time because, as Sydney was the first to point out, I was very privileged to be learning a new craft under his expert guidance.

Indeed, what he said in his arrogance was true. As I went along reading scripts, discussing them with authors and producers, and watching them being translated into action by directors, designers, lighting men, not to mention actors, I began to learn something of the craft of playwriting. In three years I even managed to write three original plays of my own. Apart from *Small Fish are Sweet*, there was *Pig's Ear with Flowers*, starring Isa Miranda and Harry Corbett, and *Roll on Bloomin' Death*, again with Corbett supported by Philip Locke and an excellent cast. All three plays did very well in terms of viewer ratings[1] and, what was more important to me, they received favourable notices.

As for Sydney's and my relationship, it was in a savage and desperate sort of way a thing of comedy. He, the old North American pro with all the box-office answers, and I, the tyro with (in my opinion) taste, discernment and integrity, fought a running battle every day of our lives. Not that we were not fond of each other. We became great friends in a perverse sort of way, and at the time of writing, we are still. But, to give an example, the afternoon after the triumphant screening of my first play, I went to Sydney with two beautiful reviews in the evening papers. I suppose I expected a pat on the head, but I should have known better. Making a sneering noise, American-style, he brushed them aside saying, 'Get wise, Pete. Last night's play is as dead as yesterday's newspaper.'

On another occasion I had been up literally all night rewriting scenes for a play (well below the usual Armchair Theatre standard) which for some emergency reason had to be rushed into rehearsal at 10.30 a.m. the following morning. When Clara came in to call me and get my breakfast I was just pinning the final sheets together. I bathed and shaved and drove out to the studios in a sort of numb daze. 'I've done it, Syd,' I said, 'but it's bloody well killed me.'

'Well, all I can say, Pete,' Sydney replied, 'is the morticians have done a great job.'

[1] They were all in the 'Top Ten' according to TAM ratings.

But after three years the unrelenting scramble to meet deadline after deadline and still produce good material (Gustave Field had by this time returned to the States) had become so oppressive that I felt I had to get away even though I could not afford to do so. I was sick of nurturing other writers' talents and pandering to their egos. What I needed was peace – time to allow my mind to breathe – and just enough money to get on a bit with some writing of my own. Furthermore a talented young man called James Roose-Evans, who was engaged in establishing the Hampstead Theatre Club, had asked me to write a play for him. We discussed various subjects without coming to any conclusion. Then one day he said, 'Have you ever heard of a writer called Rolfe?'

'Of course,' I replied. 'He invested my father as Grand Master of the Order Sanctissima Sophia.'

'Well, then . . .' said Jimmie.

'Well, then what?' I said.

'Hadrian the Seventh, of course.'

'Yes,' I said, 'of course.'

But it was not allowed to happen right away.

17

'Cunnilingus – yum, yum!' reads the legend in fine cursive script on the lavatory wall.

Back in the drill-hall where the rehearsal is taking place I sip my slot-machine coffee out of a limp paper mug and look round the cast. Who could possibly be the author of such an inspired graffito?

The ladies I rule out since even the butch sapphist in the double-breasted reefer would scarcely presume to use the men's urinal. As to the men, the juvenile lead is probably an analphabetic – certainly not a Latinist. The other slightly older man gives the impression of being educated but, I am informed, prefers fellatio as a pastime, so he must be ruled out too. The obvious choice seems to be our 'heavy', an ebullient Hiberno-Australian in his late forties and a conscientious gooser of production secretaries and make-up girls. Yes, he must be the odds-on favourite. And yet . . . 'Cunnilingus – yum, yum!' It doesn't quite have the sound of a man who likes a straight bit of nooky with the Shielas. The only other member of the company, Frank Watkins, is above suspicion. He is an old gentleman with a sweet smile who specializes in the male equivalent of 'Little-Old-Lady' parts. Besides he has been sitting quietly in a corner all the morning doing a crossword.

I become aware of the telephone ringing distantly. The floor manager pads over. 'Sydney Newman for you, Peter.' Skirting the rehearsal floor on tip-toe, I get three-quarters of the way to the call-box when I realize I have left my pencil behind. Rather than create a disturbance by going back I beg the loan of a biro from old Frank Watkins.

No need for notes, however. Sydney wants to see me. 'Come on over right away, Pete, and get the lead out of your pants.' So much the better. Three days ago I decided to resign and I have been trying ever since to get hold of Sydney, who suffers from occupational St Vitus dance, to tell him so.

190

This, therefore, is the moment I have been looking forward to. Not only am I over-worked and under-paid, but I am even denied a screen credit. Our programme is now a big national success for which Sydney gets, and hangs on to, all the kudos. He deserves much but he is not entitled to it all. Well, I think he will now at last realize just how indispensable I am. My resignation should cause a flutter in the dove-cote; perhaps even provoke an offer of more money – which last I intend to refuse.

I murmur to the production secretary that I have been called away and then cross over to give back old Frank Watkins's ball-point pen.

'How's it going?' I whisper, indicating the crossword.

'Quaite naicely, thank you,' he pipes in his tremulous tenor, 'but, I'm a tainy bit stuck with eleven across.' He reads out the clue: 'Country matters Assyrian style – nine letters. I feel it must be CUNIFORM, but that is only eight.'

'But,' I say, 'can't it also be spelt CUNEIFORM? That would make it nine.'

I pick up the paper to get a closer look. It is covered in his permutations and experiments. Then I see it: 'Cuniform' written in the identical cursive hand as the obscenity on the lavatory wall.

*   *   *

'Gee, Pete,' says Sydney as soon as I get into his office, 'I feel sick to the stomach.'

'I'm so sorry, Sydney,' I sympathize.

'Siddown and stop being such a goddam polite English schmuck.'

'But I'm not an Eng – ' I start to say.

'You are and shuddup. Listen. You heard about Wally?'

'No,' I say, 'except that he's scheduled to direct the next show.'

'Like hell he is. You know he didn't want to do it, Peter. He didn't like the script, Peter. He said the script was the lousiest bit of burnt-leatherwork he ever read. You know that?'

'Yes,' I say, 'I know he wasn't too keen on it.'

' "Not too keen on it". ' Sydney does a hopeless imitation of my English accent. 'You goddam Limeys make me sick with your lousy understatements. Wally didn't wanna do that script so badly he just smashed himself up in his goddam car. I guess that's just about the most psychosomatic motor accident I ever heard.'

I start to digest this disastrous bit of news – disastrous for the schedule rather than for Wally who I feel sure will come to no real harm. He never does. I am in the middle of a quick assessment of the repercussions when the telephone rings. Sydney picks it up.

'Hullo,' he yodels. His voice is a voice of moonshine gift-wrapped as sun.

'Hullo, Mario, how are you this morning. . . . Oh! Oh, I see. . . . Now, Mario, listen. . . . Look, Mario. . . . Now don't be like that, Mario. . . . Now, Mario, just wait a minute. . . . Look, Mario, you're a sweet, intelligent, reasonable guy and you know I have every confidence in you so just hold on to everything till I get over to the goddam studio.'

He puts down the telephone and assumes his sick-to-the-stomach look again. 'That lousy, irresponsible, hysterical schnook! Gee, I hate that guy.'

'Now what's the matter, Syd?' I ask, beginning to hate Mario as much as Wally for coming between me and my resignation.

'Matter? That goddam neurotic fag has chosen now – two days before transmission – to tell me he's running five minutes over time. C'mon, we've got to get over there quick before Katie walks off the set. You know how much it cost to hire that broad?'

When we get to rehearsal we find the junior members of the cast huddled together in the far corner of the room. Katie, the leading lady, is stalking up and down in the centre of the floor like a lioness in season. Mario and his friend the author, Adrian Worthington, wearing identical clothes and hair-styles, are standing together – twin Joans of Arc prepared to go to the stake rather than recant. The only other protagonist in this *tableau vivant* is the production assistant, poor dear, who is trying to administer cups of hot, sweet tea which nobody wants to drink.

Mario and Adrian have obviously worked each other up into a *folie à deux* and by the time Sydney and I arrive on the set they have reached a point of no return.

'Absolutely no more cuts,' they siss in unison.

Mario has his reputation to think of, he says. He is not going to be made a laughing-stock in the profession by Sydney or any-body else. No. After all, he says, he is, if nothing else, known for his artistic integrity. The trouble is that television producers assume that artists work for love and have no need of money. He doesn't want to think of Sydney as just another cynical exploiter of artists and therefore if Sydney cares to make an *ex gratia* payment in addition to the agreed fee. . . .

Adrian absolutely entirely agrees with Mario. It is nothing less than rape, he says. So far as he, Adrian, is concerned he has already cut the script to the bare bone to the detriment of its artistic merit and not another single solitary word will he cut. He would rather take his name off the credits! In any case his agent is going to claim an additional fee for the re-writes he has had to do. After all it is because Mario and he are artists that they understand and appreciate money.

Everyone knows, they chorus, that the only reason Katie has not walked off the set is because, being an artiste herself, she can appreciate artistic integrity in others. A cut of one more line, they assure us, and not even the company's lawyers will be able to keep her from walking out. After all, what's a tatty TV contract to a star?

'Okay, you guys, you win,' says Sydney, putting an avuncular arm round the two of them and smiling his lovable Genghis Khan smile. 'I'll tell the programme controller you'll be running five minutes over – but only because you're a coupla sweet guys.' He looks from one to the other exuding benign paternalism.

'Now promise me faithfully, fellers, this won't happen again, huh? No more over-runs, eh?'

Unmollified, Mario and Adrian stand silent and – apart from the odd involuntary wriggle – still. Only their lips, puckered like prunes, indicate how bitterly they resent the fact that they have failed to precipitate a scene.

'What a couple of goddam lousy jerks,' says Sydney, putting on his blood-bath face as the padded studio doors close behind us. 'Remind me to fry in hell before I renew their contracts. Right?'

'Right!' I say.

'Right!'

We run straight into Rosie. Part of Rosie's stock-in-trade as

Casting Director is a ladylike, twin-set-and-pearls charm. But now her face, normally rigged to accommodate the most petulant artiste, is like a hopeless dawn.

'Oh, thank goodness I've found you, Sydney, dear. Could I possibly have a quick word – ' she smiles a pained apology at me – 'in private?'

'Sure, darling, sure,' says Sydney, putting his arm round Rosie's waist. 'Pardon us a minute, Pete, willya?'

'Of course, Sydney,' I say, 'but there is something of the utmost importance I must talk to you about as soon as you're free.'

'Sure, sure. Later, okay?'

Back in my own office I start to work myself up into a rage: a rage of frustration and disappointment. My decision to resign has for the last few days buoyed me up with a sense of freedom and power. Now this feeling of elation is being whittled away by just those circumstances from which I passionately wish to break free. For the third time I fail to get Sydney on the telephone.

Then my bell rings and I hear the voice of Sydney's secretary saying: 'Oh, Peter, thank goodness I've found you! Sydney's been going mad looking for you. Will you come to his office right away, please?'

'You bet I will,' I say venomously. '*I* want to see *him*.'

'Sydney,' I begin before even shutting his office door. 'There's something I'm going to – '

'Peter,' says Sydney, looking at me as if he has just received the news of a close bereavement. 'Forgive me, but not now, eh? This is something very important.'

'What I have to say is important too,' I reply in my most disagreeable manner.

'Peter, I detect a shrill note in your voice. Come on, Pete, we're friends, you and I, aren't we?'

'Yes, I suppose so,' I admit reluctantly.

'You're a great guy, Pete. The greatest. You know I always rely on you. Now there's something you can do that would be a very great help to me personally.'

'What is it?' I say in sulky voice.

'Pete, Rosie's in a very awkward spot, Pete, and I guess this is

194

something only you can handle. You see it's awkward for Rosie being a woman, but you being an English gennelman, you'd know how to handle it.'

'Sydney,' I say, 'I don't mind how much you insult me, but for God's sake stop calling me an English gentleman. The last time you said it I agreed to a cut in salary.'

'Aw, forget it. What you're getting now is peanuts. When I take you back to Hollywood I'll make you the richest gonoph in the business. Think big, Peter, think big.'

'All right,' I say, 'I'm thinking big, what is it?'

'Well, I guess a guy from Eton would have just the right touch with this, Pete. You see there's a bit of trouble in Henry's show right now. You know who he's cast in the lead?'

'Yes,' I reply, 'Valerie Playfair.'

'No, I mean the guy to play opposite her.'

'Yes, it's that aggressive bastard who calls himself a "method" actor. Tim Halloran.'

'Yeah, yeah, Tim Halloran, that's it. Well, Valerie – gee, that girl's a sweetie; I'd like to give her a shtup just to show my appreciation. . . .'

'Come to the point, Sydney,' I say.

'Peter,' says Sydney, 'Valerie is very, very upset. She's complained to Henry and Henry's complained to Rosie. Poor Rosie, she was so embarrassed when she told me. Well, it seems like every time Valerie and this guy, Tim, have to kiss on camera – you know what Henry is: all that neo-realism shit – well, it seems this Tim Halloran gets too goddam intimate. From what Rosie tells me each time – well, he kinda commits an indecent assault. Now you know the directors of this company, Peter – lawyers, church-wardens, nonconformists. They don't like that sort of thing. They're very sensitive guys, Peter. Remember how they hated that transvestite murder story? They've got to think about the Queen's Birthday.'

'Of course they have. I'd quite forgotten.'

'Swell, Pete. Now you just get along and have a quiet word with Tim.'

*　　*　　*

That was an hour ago. I am now sitting in my office dabbing at a cut and swollen lip while the fool floor-manager administers second-rate first aid and fills me in on Tim Halloran's boxing career before he was 'discovered' by Theatre Workshop. Mercifully the telephone interrupts and I hear the familiar voice of the girl: 'Peter, Sydney Newman for you.'

The oedomatose condition of my lower lip tends to muffle my acid reply.

'Pete,' says Sydney, as if he were about to invest me with a Purple Heart. 'Gee, Pete,' he says, 'you sure cut the mustard with Tim Halloran. He just thinks you're the greatest for standing up to him like that. Did you know he'd been a professional prize-fighter?'

'I didn't know at the time otherwise you can bet your bottom dollar, or whatever you use for money where you come from, I wouldn't have gone,' I say, as viciously as I can under the circumstances.

'Well, that's the "method" for you . . . Hey, would you come down to my office a moment? How about a drink, huh?'

'Yes, I could do with the drink,' I say, 'and there's something I have to say.'

Now's the time to spring it on him. Wait till he sees my lip. I'll make the sentimental old bastard wriggle a bit. I began to feel more kindly towards Halloran and the 'method'.

Sydney greets me with two outstretched hands and his most loving expression. 'Pete, old man, you're the greatest. In all sincerity – and I'm telling you the honest truth – you behaved just like I'd expect an English gennelman to behave.'

I groan theatrically.

'Have a drink, old man,' he says.

Glass in hand, his manner suddenly changes. He starts to look at me like a wounded bull-moose. 'Peter,' he says, before I can get my swollen lip to the glass. 'Something very sad has happened, Peter, something very, very sad.'

Unaffected by any sadness but my own, I let him carry on.

'It's Harry Bates,' he says.

Harry Bates is one of our writers, an earnest young man convinced he is writing for suffering humanity. In consequence most of his stuff is unusable since the greater part of it is abuse of whatever he regards as the Establishment. His last two works were banned by the censor because they respectively undermined public confidence in the RSPCA and in the Trustees of the National Gallery.

Following his first success about corruption in the Metropolitan Police Force which caused questions to be asked in the House, he gave up a steady job as a precision grinder in a machine-tool factory, married one of our production assistants, bought himself a corduroy jacket, and set up as a full-time writer. Since then not one of his scripts has reached the screen. Now his wife, Sylvia, is in the family way and funds in the Bates's home are running low.

This is nothing unusual for a young writer but after Sydney, with real reluctance, turned down the last script, 'Perjured Pulpit', Harry began to feel he wasn't wanted. This manifested itself in the writing of a number of abusive letters addressed to myself and other small fry. The last one, however, accusing the Company of cowardice, hedonism, toadying to vested interests and conspiring to keep the bread out of a good Marxist's mouth, was addressed to Sydney himself with a copy to the Chairman of the Board of Directors. Bates then apparently pawned his typewriter and retired to his basement to await martyrdom.

Unfortunately, Sydney, having agreed with the Chairman that it was rather a 'silly' letter, forgot all about it. And so the weeks went by with Harry Bates feeling more and more unwanted owing to the non-arrival of his executioners, and with Sydney Newman, the Grand Inquisitor, remaining oblivious to his predicament.

It then seems that Harry, having neither religion nor sense of humour to support him in the hour of need, took to his bed and pulled the covers over his head. After he had been there a week refusing to speak to anybody, Sylvia came round and wept on Sydney's shoulder. That was what she had just finished doing when I came in.

'Gee, Pete,' says Sydney, sentimentally shaking his woolly head, 'just imagine that poor guy! Lying there day after day with his face turned to the wall.'

'Tough,' I say as best I can through the swollen lip.

'Gee, Pete, it sure is. There he is just lying there. And he won't talk. He won't talk to anybody, not even to Sylvia. Goddamit! What did that sweet kid have to get mixed up with that schmuck for?'

'Well, that's the way things go,' I say trying to make light of the whole thing. 'Now there's something extremely important I've been trying all day to. . . .'

'Day after day with his face turned to the wall. Just try and imagine that, Peter.'

'Yes, I'll try,' I say. 'Now what I have to say is this. . . .'

'You know we've got to do something for that guy, Pete. Maybe he's a jerk but he's a human being, Pete, and he's suffering.'

'Yes,' I say, 'so am I – together with fifty million Chinese.'

'Peter, I don't like you when you're cynical,' Sydney says wagging his enormous head. 'I thought you were bigger than that. I thought you had a heart, Peter. In fact I know you have, or I wouldn't ask this thing of you. Now listen, I want you to get along right now – take my car if you like, Peter – get along right now to where this jerk lives and get him out of his goddam bed. Get him out of bed, Peter and tell him Sydney Newman's never let down any one of his lousy writers yet. Tell him the writer is the most important guy in the business. Tell him I said so. Well, Pete, what say?'

'I didn't say anything, Sydney.'

'What? This isn't like you, Peter. Where's your humanity? Where's your nobility? Where's your English sense of fair play?'

'Sydney,' I roar, 'don't give me that old-fashioned Hollywood shit. You're not Irving Thalberg and I'm not Scott Fitzgerald. I don't give a fart for Harry Bates and his asinine predicament, and as far as I'm concerned the longer he stays in bed without a typewriter the better.'

'Now wait a minute, Peter. . . .'

'Sydney, you're going to hear me out,' I yell, trying desperately to keep the *tremolo agitato* out of my voice. 'I've come here to resign!'

'Resign? You're not serious, Peter – or are ya?'

'I'm deadly serious, Sydney,' I say.

'Gee, Peter, I'm sorry . . . I'm gonna miss you, Peter.'

'You will like hell,' I say.

'Now don't *be* like that, Peter.'

There is a short pause and I watch with objective interest a variety of practical thoughts pass through the big head whose face just fails to convince with its expression of hurt surprise. Suddenly he changes it to the more familiar one of dynamic enthusiasm.

'Hey, how about this for a great idea?' He gives me a big stage wink as he flicks up the inter-com to his secretary. 'Say, darling,' he says, 'get me Harry Bates, sweetheart. Yeah, Harry Bates.'

Sydney then turns to me with a look of childlike naïvety. 'Say, Peter,' he says with a hand over the mouth-piece, 'that guy owes us a lot of dough on that *Prick in the Pulpit* script. What a dog! How much are you earning now, Peter?'

I mentioned a trifling sum.

'But that guy's hungry, Peter. I guess he'll take maybe half.'

The telephone buzzes and Sydney picks it up. 'Hullo, Harry, ole man,' Sydney carols like a chorus of spring daffodils, 'I've got the greatest job waiting here for you, Harry,' he says. 'I'm sending my car. Can you come on over right away?'

18

To reach the Lambourne Downs from Hungerford the simplest way is to drive out in a north-westerly direction and cross the River Kennet at Chilton Foliat. Half-way through the village is a road that rises steeply right-handed up a wooded hill past Straight Soley Farm to Inholmes. Near the top of the hill is a left turn by some knapped flint cottages which takes one for about half a mile along a narrow lane hedged with well-grown hollies. Near the end of this lane, which runs parallel to a Roman road called Ermin Street, and which is in fact the saddle of a long ridge between the valley of the Kennet and the Lambourne river, there is a cottage whose thatch, on its northern side, goes down to within a foot or two of the ground. This is Ragnals Cottage, and it is here that I now live.

Ragnals was sold to me for the friendly price of one hundred pounds by John Gilbey of Inholmes on whose estate on the Berkshire-Wiltshire border it stands. It is a lonely cottage and that is a great part of its charm because it is, in feeling as well as in fact, a long, long way from Piccadilly, Leicester Square, Crutchéd Friars, Battersea Bridge Road, and a great many other places in a Metropolis that has long since lost any magic it may once have held for me. Further, since I have no telephone, my privacy can neither be invaded by the mandatory calls of Sydney Newman, nor by the arbitrary penetrations of Frederika Maxwell. I have come here to lick my wounds and to hole up in solitude until they are healed.

The last and most material injury was inflicted on me indirectly and without malice by Declan Papadopoulos.

When Anne and Louis got married and went to live in the Alpes Maritimes, and when the Fields returned to Malibu, California, the good life at Albert Studios came to an end and, apart from the pleasant ambience, there was not much point in being there any more. I would have stayed, however, but for the fact that two responsible people who should – and did – know better, involved me in litigation with my landlady as a result of which my lease was not renewed. Musketeer Papadopoulos then came to the rescue and offered house-room, which is to say he rented me a room in his spacious Chelsea flat.

'He was a charlatan rather than a crook, a man of immense energy and wide emotion, fuelled by vanity, forcing his way into the counsels of the great by wit and trickery and tumbling out of them through his insensate sexual appetite.' So Cyril Connolly describes Casanova, but it is also an almost perfect description of Declan Papadopoulos, though I must add that Declan mitigates this obloquy by having a sense of humour, by being good company, and by being generous, as they say, to a fault. He is also touchingly optimistic and is always ready to embark with the greatest enthusiasm on any new scheme until the cigar, so to speak, blows up in his face – or someone else's.

Declan has dominated more dinner-table conversations *in absentia* than anyone else I know. I say *in absentia* because, rather than ask Declan to dinner (to which there are always certain hazards), people often prefer to arrange a dinner-party in order to discuss him.

In appearance Declan resembles pictures of Honoré de Balzac and, like Balzac, he has invented his own personal myth. In fact Declan is a mythomane *par excellence* and, in the grip of any one of them, he becomes lost to the world of reality. For example, I have been at a party with Declan when, in my hearing – and knowing it to be in my hearing – he has told three different people three different lies about himself: notably that during the war he was (i) in a famous Highland Regiment, (ii) in the Irish Guards, and (iii) in SOE (a 'subversive activities' organization) by whom he was dropped by parachute into Occupied France, to be captured by the Nazis and tortured. In the grip of this last fiction he sometimes puts on a limp.

But I happened to know – and he knows that I know – that he was in a Line regiment where he seduced his Colonel's daughter and was forced to marry her at Bren gun-point. That was the nearest he ever came to seeing a shot fired in anger. But the interesting thing is that he allows me to overhear such stories which, to say the least, lack what film-makers call 'continuity'. It seems, then, that in the throes of his own mythology, Declan casts aside all caution and pride, which is probably a symptom of this rather innocent disease by which his life is governed.

Having said all this I am grateful for having Declan in my life; so much so that when the time came to make the move, the prospect of good times to come with him did much to compensate for the loss of my studio.

All went well at first. I was busy writing and my industry in this respect encouraged Declan for a while to continue with some literary work of his own. In the domestic sphere, though messy in the kitchen, he is one of the best amateur cooks in London, and in consequence we had a number of enjoyable soirées, though this meant of course that we spent more money on wine and food than either of us could afford. One day apparently our next door neighbour had ordered a couple of dozen bottles of claret from his wine merchant. The delivery man mistakenly left them equidistant between our two doors and Declan, who also was expecting – or perhaps I should say, hoping for – a delivery of wine, took them in. It was not until we were down to the last couple of bottles that the neighbour realized a mistake had been made.

My brain works best in the morning so that when I am trying to write I like to get to bed before midnight. Sometimes I would be woken in the early hours by girlish laughter and sounds of merriment from Declan's part of the flat. The next morning I would hear him groaning in the bath as, soaking in the hot water, he lay tortured by his conscience or, perhaps, by purely physical pain. Whatever the cause, the groans were loud and pitiful to hear. They were the sounds of Declan, the real man, naked and alone.

Declan's daytime activities, whatever they were, tended to keep him out of the house and I was, therefore, left alone to get on with my work. At least, I was for a time. Then two men began to call. The first time I simply told them that Declan was out, and that was that. I thought no more about it. But by about their third visit I began to get irritated. After all, who likes to be interrupted at his work? The fourth time the two men came – they were always the same ones – they started by asking me who I was. What the hell was it to do with them? I became angry and even rude. When Declan came back that night I asked him irritably how the devil he expected me to get on with my work when I was constantly being badgered by his callers.

Callers? What callers? Why hadn't I mentioned them before? Declan now became extremely alert and, after questioning me closely as to the nature of the inquiries and my responses to them, he disappeared into the next room where for about half an hour I heard his typewriter clacking away. When he came back he presented me with a handful of receipts, all ante-dated, amounting to the entire contents of his flat.

'It's all yours, old boy,' he said. 'You bought it all off me, understand? Now I must be off. I may be in Ireland for a while, but I'll keep in touch. Help yourself to anything left in the cellar and have a good time.' He gave me an affectionate pat on the arm, picked up an old and bulging briefcase and disappeared into the night.

For the next few days I got on with the television programme I was writing and did not think too much about Declan or his visitors. Then one day they came back. This time they asked me straight out who owned the contents of the flat. Remembering Declan's injunctions, I said rather haughtily that I did.

'Quite so, sir,' said the leading bumbailiff. 'My colleague and I are Officers of the Court, and we hold a writ issued against you, Mr-er-Luke, isn't it? – on behalf of various parties claiming certain debts. Do you follow me so far, sir?'

Miserably, I had to agree that I did. The obscene fellow then slapped a buff envelope into my hand and made the following speech:

'The position is that, in brief, the Court has seen fit to award against you the initial sum of the debt plus the costs of the several Plaintiffs versus Yourself for which a remittance must be made into Court forthwith in default of which and in consideration of a Warrant of Execution there will be no alternative but to attend at your premises and remove the contents thereof for sale by Public Auction.'

So that's it, I thought. 'All for one . . .' and me with an overdraft at the bank, behind with my payments to Lettice, and Declan, for all I knew, in his hammock and a thousand miles away. I quickly telephoned round London but not one of our mutual acquaintance had seen hide nor hair of him. I even telephoned to one or two people in Ireland which at first raised hopes. With the usual Irish desire to please they thought that he had been seen going into a pub in Baggott Street with Jack Doyle's wife, putting a monkey on a loser at Leopardstown races, driving Siobhan Mackenna round the ring of Kerry, making a barefoot pilgrimage to Lough Derg, entertaining Monsignor Paddy Browne and 'The Bird' Flanagan to lunch at Jammet's, and so on. But when finally I put them to the hard question, they admitted that they had no idea where he was at all.

I will now cut through the fatiguing minutiae of the next few weeks and come to the action. I was summonsed to attend at the Law Courts at a certain date to appear before Judge in Chambers. The days passed. Then the day before the hearing Declan suddenly appeared again. He had somehow heard all about it.

After making the friendliest apologies for his absence, but at the same time rather skilfully making light of the inconvenience I had been put to, he set about to reassure me.

'It'll be quite all right, old boy. Just stick to the story. That's all you have to do. I've already briefed Babington-Smith (his friend and lawyer) who'll be with you in Court just in case you feel lonely. You will understand that obviously I can't appear in Court myself' – and here he burst into hearty laughter in which he expected me to join – 'but I shall be with you in spirit' – here he convulsed again – 'in the pub across the road drinking your health.'

And so the day came. Bolstered by Declan's assurances that there were really no problems at all, I went along with a lightish heart. It got a bit heavier, however, when I saw that the Court was packed with wigs and gowns all apparently representing the 'Other Side'. Nor was I much encouraged by Declan's solicitor when he finally showed up. He seemed very distrait and kept looking at his watch saying that he hoped the Judge would not keep us too long. I hoped so too, but probably for different reasons. When the Judge did finally come, and everybody had stood up and had sat down again, my courage was distinctly low. His Lordship then spent a long time filling, emptying, and refilling an elaborate sort of fountain pen. He reminded me of P. A. Stamford, the school bully. Then the moment came.

'Raise the Bible in the right hand and repeat after me I swear by Almighty God that I shall speak the truth and the whole truth and nothing but the truth so help me God you may sit down.'

What happened during the next few hours – I can't remember even roughly how many – was what is generally known as a waking nightmare, while I stuttered and sweated, and finally listened, as the Other Side drove a coach-and-horses through the whole sorry fabric of our hopeless lie.

At the end the Judge, screwing the cap back on his fat fountain pen, found in favour of the Plaintiffs and ordered the Defendant (me) to pay the full amount of the debts plus costs. He ended his peroration by saying that he had been tempted to put the file in the hands of the Director of Public Prosecutions to investigate it as a case of flagrant perjury, but that he had refrained from doing so since he was inclined to think that the Defendant (me) had now learnt a salutary lesson.

As Counsel for the Other Side shuffled their papers and made dates for games of golf, I saw the pusillanimous Babington-Smith trying to look as if the verdict was only what could have been expected. I cut him dead and made straight for the pub across the road. There I downed two large brandies at Declan's expense without speaking. Then I gave it to him straight. I said every nasty thing that I had ever felt, or heard said, about him and at the end of it he was looking so contrite, and was indeed so sincerely apologetic, that I took pity on him. I took him to the best restaurant in London and stood him lunch with the last few quid I possessed.

19

'Darling, there is a grasshopper in the winter jasmin.' It was the day after the Court fiasco and I was talking on the telephone to Jane Bomford who lives with her husband, Jimmy (farmer, art collector, and occasional genius), in Wiltshire on the high ground between Aldbourne and Ogbourne St George.

'. . . and all the hedgehogs are dead, darling. They ate the "Slug Death". It is so sad but I can't allow the slugs to eat my *Mekanopsis Balii* – the blue is so much finer than the *Ipomea*. I've only lost two – and one was the gardener's child. You can't have a beautiful garden with slugs – or children, darling.'

Jane has her own idea of priorities in this life and the problems of hedgehogs, children, and a friend who has just made a perfect fool of himself, rate low compared to the health of *Mekanopsis Balii*. I would not necessarily argue with this, nor would I wish to since it was the Bomfords who were responsible for my finding Ragnal Cottage.

After the Papadopoulos débâcle, I gratefully decided to accept the Arts Council grant of £100 which, if I went down to Ragnals and lived frugally, might support me for long enough to write the play of *Hadrian the Seventh* for Jimmie Roose-Evans. So within two days of being permitted to walk a free man out of the Law Courts I piled all my things into the back of a Bedford van and set off to take possession of the only piece of real estate that I have ever owned. Declan and I bid one another an affectionate farewell and as I set out down the Bath Road his assurances that he 'would take care of everything' were ringing encouragingly in my ears.

The cottage, when I moved in, was much as Enoch Mackerel had left it when, some two or three years earlier, he had been taken into a Home. Nocky was an amiable old solitary of variable sanity who camped, rather than lived in, what was in effect a ruin. Upstairs there were a few old sacks where he slept on the frame of an iron bedstead which, in default of springs, was lashed criss-cross with string. Below there was an upturned tea-chest on which lay a chipped tin mug and a verdigrised fork with one broken tine. On the floor by the chimney, and dry as a rusk, was a dead jackdaw, and against the wall a pile of rubble thrown up by a gang of mice.

In all, the little place had rising damp, mice in the wainscote, rats in the lath-and-plaster, starlings in the thatch, jackdaws in the chimney, and one could see a wide expanse of sky through the roof – a normal enough state of affairs in a deserted house in the country. Nocky Mackerel must have found it pretty hard lying, though nobody could say truly that he lived alone.

However, there was no worm in the timbers and for my taste the advantages were enormous. To the north the far side of the lane was lined with old elms, of which one giant in particular seemed to be the guardian of the house. On the near side was a magnificent hedge of holly, and round by the porch stood an ancient yew which, judging by the size of its sienna bole, was about as old as St Paul's Cathedral. In the little paddock were three crab-apple trees and a fine greengage and, at the bottom of it, an ivy-covered privy with a view that travelled, in a gentle slope of arable land, here and there indented with tree-grown chalk pits, down to Wiltshire Bottom, to rise again in the distance of the next county to Crooked Soley and Marridge Hill. I doubt if there was a better view – as views from privies go – in all England.

It was a view that stretched my eyes, eyes which had for so long been cramped in city streets and which ached from the ugliness of them. It was a view my eyes had longed for, and for it I would have put up with much more – even with piles from sitting too long over a draughty hole. As to holes, there was the one in the roof. But when Jane told him of my plight, Jimmy Bomford of his goodness rethatched the whole thing so that it was bright yellow the whole summer long, and even the sparrows took a little time to make themselves at home in it.

And so I came to live at Ragnals with no more than £100 in the bank and scarcely any prospects whatsoever.

When one lives quite alone in a remote part of the country one soon develops a new set of perceptions and sensibilities, not unlike those of an infantry soldier in war. Yesterday evening I was sitting at my desk working when I was startled by a noise in the next room. I jumped up to find out what it was. At first I saw nothing. And then as I stood poised, all senses alert, it happened again. The yellow petals of an overblown rose were falling like an avalanche on to the table.

One can also become a little unhinged. One bluebottle can interrupt my work for up to ten minutes, or until such time as I have killed it. The sparrows that chirrup and bicker in the roof can drive me into such a passion that I find myself blasting into my own thatch with a twelve-bore gun. As for the rats and mice, I devote hours to cunning and vindictive plans for trapping and poisoning them. Once a screech-owl settled in the yew tree and gave me twenty minutes of its voice at top pitch between one and two in the morning. I gave it two barrels of 'number seven' shot. The noise of the explosions was fearful. And suddenly I saw myself, a demented creature, white and naked in the pale moonlight, with a smoking shot-gun in my hands.

But there are beautiful noises as well: the rich round flute of the bullfinch, for example, has a call that matches in sweetness the roseate colour of its breast. At dusk and dawn the cock-cocking of the pheasants and the whickering of partridges fill the air with clean percussive sounds. And after dark the peewits still continue to cry as they flap and flicker over the night fields while, in the elms, the wind stirs the top branches into a gentle sibilance.

Sometimes when the wind gets up and tears at the high trees, it feels like a storm at sea, it is so great, so strong, so powerful. How can this roof, or even the great elms, withstand it? But when the wind is still, the moon rises swiftly so that it seems to make the earth spin on its axis under my feet. It is then that the badgers come out of their holts in the chalk pits, and the owls in Carols Wood hoot at the field mice, and the roebuck dare to cross the road. Then it seems that we all revolve like tumblers, man, beast, vegetable, artefact in this high firmament of an elm-hung, bat-ridden, moonstruck, barley night. And then when dawn comes the moon recedes, an old bowl of polished rosewood, leaving the yellow crab-apples lying glistening in the dew.

And so the months go by, spring passes into summer and the fields changed from green to yellow, yellow to brown: cocks grow spurs and the leverets come to hare's estate. One day a hen partridge brought her brood cheepering from the wheatfield into the paddock and past my workroom window. Act 1 was written and Act 2 was nearly done: summer was over and autumn was on its way. Another month's work and I could take a complete first draft up to London for the men of affairs to read.

I returned from Aldbourne one day, having carried out a successful raid on the Bomford's vegetable garden, when I was stopped by a man I knew who did occasional jobs of hedging and ditching for Farmer Bracey.

'There was a gentleman here looking for you this morning,' he said. This was a considerable surprise because normally I do not see anybody except the postman from week's beginning to week's end. If it had been anybody like John Gilbey or Noel Blatchley (the local horse psychiatrist) he would have mentioned them by name. I puzzled about it for a bit and then forgot the matter completely.

From a writer's point of view the main disadvantage to living alone is that there is nobody with whom to discuss problems of work. Writing plays is a crude business compared to the finer aspects of the art of letters, and I think the person who writes them is properly called a playwright – like a shipwright or a wheelwright – because he has to perform a very exact craft which either works successfully or not at all. If a boat has a loose plank it sinks. If a wheel is not round it comes off. If a play is not sound it comes off too.

They say that the last act of a play is the most difficult one. I would not necessarily endorse this, but I was now at a stage where I had come up against a variety of snags and it would have been a help and a relief, and possibly even a solution, if I could have discussed them with someone in the profession.

I had reached this point one day when, rather than continue to beat my head against the typewriter, I decided to go out and get some fresh air. A neighbour had lent me a crow-bar and needed it back.

On my return I saw a black Reading taxi parked in the lane. Going round to the front of the cottage I came face to face with an unpleasant-looking individual wearing one of those grey-green suits worn by professional people in country towns. He made haste to identify himself. He was a Mr Gladwell of 13, The Market, Reading, a member of the Certificated Bailiffs Association representing the Sheriff of London. In short he was a bum and had come to destrain my entire effects for non-payment into Court of the amount of Declan's debt plus costs as awarded against me by the Judge in Chambers. Declan, despite all his assurances that he would 'take care of everything', had taken care of nothing but himself. This time it was not just money that they wanted, but my cottage and everything I possessed.

A bailiff's job cannot be a pleasant one, but then nobody with the slightest sense of decency would ever undertake it. I would rather be a lavatory attendant than spend my time hounding and bullying people who have got themselves into trouble and cannot afford to pay.

I think that what used to be called an 'Oxford accent' superimposed upon poverty and misfortune brings out a sadistic impulse in people like this Mr Gladwell. Certainly in my case he was determined to add insult to injury. He was, presumably, perfectly within his rights to look round the cottage in order to assess the value of the contents. Moreover it was true that I had furnished the place from odd stuff picked up at local auctions. But it was also true that I had one or two good things; among them a fine Le Brocquy painting. So Mr Gladwell showed not only malevolence but ignorance when, looking at Louis's 'Citrus Fruit', which had recently been in a major exhibition of his work, he said, 'All a load of old rubbish, isn't it?'

Then, having left me in no doubt as to my predicament, he taxied back to Reading at my expense.

As soon as he had disappeared out of sight I went straight to the typewriter, tore out the existing page of H.VII, Act 2, Sc.3, inserted a piece of writing-paper, and wrote to Declan as follows:

Ragnals Cottage, Woodlands St Mary, Newbury, Berks.

Sept. 1, 1961

'My dear Declan,

'For the last fortnight neighbours have been telling me of a mysterious visitor who has called several times when I've been out. Today he called again, and I was in. The Sheriff's Officer from

Reading, acting on instructions from London, has now seized the contents of this cottage in default of payment of the following:

Andrew Lesley & Co. v Peter Luke	£115 7	4
Sheriff of London v Peter Luke	£106 10	7
Total	£221 17	11

'Having heard nothing further from you in the matter, I had foolishly assumed that these costs had been paid. I think you might have warned me. I am now being hounded by these people to see that I don't decamp. In a remote part of the country like this, where everybody knows one's business, it is very bad for me, Declan, and I do not want – cannot afford – to lose my credit round here. As you know I am not earning at present. I have my two children's school fees still to pay and I am trying to write a play against the clock. Unlike Balzac, I'm unable to concentrate on my work while under the threat of sheriffs and bailiffs. Need I say more?'

Then for four days there was complete and utter silence, during which time I tried but completely failed to get on with the play. Then came a telegram: 'COPING LETTER IN POST DECLAN'
This was followed by a letter dated September 4.

'Dear Peter,
'You will by now have received my telegram. Yours was a considerable blow to me. I hoped that the instalment arrangements suggested through Babington-Smith would have been accepted. Also the sum you mention in your letter is considerably in excess of that quoted to me by Babington-Smith. However, I will look into that and have today sent some money to B-S which should halt the Bumbailiff Brigade until I somehow raise the rest. To protect you I must raise this money and I will do so, but that is the only reason I would give a penny to these sharks. I am sorry things have disturbed your creative peace. I hear your play is finished and good.
                                        Yours, Declan.'

By the same post came a letter from Mr Gladwell's superior under the imposing superscription of Officer to the Sheriff of Berkshire.

'Dear Sir,

re: Andrew Lesley & Co – v – Yourself
The Sheriff of London – v – Yourself

'I refer to my Assistant's call upon you on Friday last, 1st instant when you were informed of the above Warrants of Execution.

'I shall be glad to receive a remittance from you made up as follows:

Andrew Lesley & Co – v – yourself	£115	7	4
Sheriff of London – v – yourself	£106	10	7
Total	£221	17	11

'Unless this amount is paid forthwith, I shall have no alternative but to attend at your premises and remove the contents for sale by Public Auction.

Yours faithfully.'

This last only aggravated the sense of insecurity engendered by Declan's letter. I went back to the typewriter.

'My dear Declan,

'Thanks for your wire and note which was not entirely reassuring. I enclose a copy from the local Sheriff's office and I am sending another copy to Babington-Smith since you tell me he didn't give you the right figures (which seems a little casual for a competent lawyer).

'I cannot sufficiently impress on you that these people mean business – and they mean business NOW. They want their money; in default of which they are going to sell me up lock, stock and barrel. They will not be fobbed off with something on account and a promise. So you must do something really drastic *ec dum*. There is no longer time for prevarication or procrastination. I will not bother you with more on this subject.

'I have only finished 1st draft of play and have major rewrites to do before 23rd of this month. I am not succeeding in getting on with my work.

Yrs,

Peter.'

At the same time I felt that Babington-Smith, despite my feelings of no confidence in either him or his profession, should know what was going on from my – as opposed to Declan's – point of view. I therefore wrote to him as follows:

'You will by now have heard of my plight from the very helpful lady in your office to whom I spoke on the telephone this afternoon. Enclosed is a self-explanatory letter (copy) from the Sheriff of Berkshire's office. These people really mean business and I have told Declan P as much in no uncertain terms. Knowing his character so well I might have known that, once the initial shock of losing the case was over, he would fail to make any effective provision against this inevitable event. I need hardly say how thoroughly I resent it.

'Is Declan now making a serious attempt to pay? I doubt if they will be put off any longer with something on account and a promise. Besides, Declan is inclined to forget his promises when it comes to substantiating them with cash. Be that as it may, I do not intend to be the Sacrificial Lamb. Unlike Declan, I have to maintain a wife and two children and I cannot pay for this folly even if I would. You may say, the more fool me for getting involved. I would agree with you. But having had my goods "seized" in two places, and having had to suffer the persecution of bailiffs and the scorn of Judge and Counsel, I think I have expiated my stupidity.

'Could I now ask you (a) to ring the Berks Sheriff's office and ask them to call off their blood-hounds and (b) make Declan see that no grown man of over forty should behave in such a childishly irresponsible way towards a friend.

'I would be very glad to hear from you at an early date to let me know how the situation stands. I am down here supposedly to write a play for production in January. This worrying business is not helping me to get on with my work.'

Having put these two long letters in Lambourn Woodlands' pillar-box, my creative energies were dissipated for the day.

On the 7th I received another telegram from Declan:

'SITUATION UNDER CONTROL BOSS BUMBAILIFF IN
NEGOTIATION RELAX AND WORK – DECLAN.'

The reply that arrived from Babington-Smith on the 8th was sympathetic but far from reassuring as to Declan's efforts and intentions. So, after three more days when the uncertainty of my position made any attempts to concentrate on work impossible, I sat down and played another tune on my typewriter.

'Thank you for your kindly intended telegram but unfortunately the circumstances attending it do not make it possible for me to "relax and work".

'You have now, I gather, offered £30 down plus £10 instalments. But I understand that the creditors' solicitors are unlikely to accept this against a debt of £222, which means that I shall be once more in the position of the tethered goat. Even if they do accept it and then, at some later date, you fail to adhere strictly to the arrangement, my persecution by the bailiffs will begin again. (I am still mystified to know how they got my address here, anyway.)

'What I want you to do now, therefore, in order to alleviate somewhat my total vulnerability in the matter, is to write me a letter acknowledging your liability to me for the sum of £221 17 11. I would like this by return of post. If you can liberate me from the responsibility for this debt you can fight the creditors in your own way. With my family commitments I cannot fight them and will only hamper you from doing so.

'Finally, I would like you to tell me what steps you propose to take to liquidate this debt in the probable event of the creditors not accepting your present offer. Have you thought of raising money on the lease of your flat? I wait to hear from you.'

Three days later Declan replied as follows:

'I have instructed and enabled Babington-Smith to settle the
Sheriff's claims at the most favourable terms he can, but to settle
them, so that you are troubled no further in any way.'

In datelining my reply, it occurred to me that, in the seventeen
days since the bailiff's first visit, owing to my natural anxiety and
the necessity to write so many letters, I had done no work on the
play at all.

'Thank you for your letter of the 15th but, alas, it means absolutely nothing (though I'm not ungrateful to you for trying to
put me at ease).
    'You must know, as I well do, that in law I am solely and
entirely responsible for your debts amounting to £222. I have no
doubt that you have "instructed" Babington-Smith but no
amount of instruction to him or any other solicitor can alter the
above fact. Only prompt settlement of your debt can get me off
the hook. That is why I must repeat the requests made in my last
letter, namely:
    '(1) I want you to write me a letter acknowledging your
liability to me for the sum of £221 17 11. This will be held, if
you like, by Babington-Smith and returned to you as soon as the
creditors have been paid.
    '(2) I would like you to tell me what steps you propose to
take to liquidate the debt in the event of your present offer being
rejected by the creditors.
    'I feel, Declan, that you have not yet seriously considered
making a personal sacrifice such as raising the money on the lease
of your flat. If I had the money I would pay this debt without
further ado, and wait for repayment when things are easier for
you. But my circumstances are probably more straitened than
yours. In the interests of a long-standing friendship I therefore
hope you will now act, and at once. I wait to hear.'

I also wrote to Babington-Smith to keep him in the picture,

a picture which was daily becoming more like one of the more sinister works by Daumier or Doré.

'Thank you for your letter of the 8th. I would be grateful if you would let me know how the position now stands with Andrew Lesley & Co. and the Sheriff of Berkshire. I have no faith in the evasive and placatory answers I get to my letters from Declan Papadopoulos. Twice bit, thrice shy. Am I still in danger of another visit from the Bailiff complete with pantechnicon and auctioneer's hammer?

'I have twice asked Declan for a letter of indemnity but so far no dice. I have suggested that if he wrote me a letter acknowledging the debt of £222, to me, I would give it to you to hold until the debt is liquidated.'

In reply came a letter from his clerk regretting the fact that Mr Babington-Smith was on holiday:

'. . . I quite understand your anxiety in relation to the above but you will, doubtless, be relieved to hear that an instalment basis has now been reached between Mr Papadopoulos and the Solicitors with the effect that the Sheriff should not worry you again provided you pay the costs incurred by the latter in the execution ie. approx £15.

'I think I should warn you, however, that should there be any default in the instalment basis (although I realize that it is not your pigeon) the Solicitors will proceed with Bankruptcy proceedings without further notice, *that is against you*.[1]

'I have asked Mr Papadopoulos to get in touch with you regarding some form of acknowledgement of the £222 and await his reply, and have also reported to him on the above.'

In view of paragraph three, I felt anything but relieved. This was in no way ameliorated by another letter from the Officer to the Sheriff of Berkshire received by the same post.

[1] My italics.

'Dear sir,
    Andrew Lesley Co. – v – Declan Papadopoulos and yourself
    'I have today received instructions from the Plaintiffs solicitors
in this matter, that the Execution levied on your furniture, can
be withdrawn upon payment of Sheriff's charged as under:

Sheriff's Poundage:	4	18	6
Levy fee:	1	11	6
Mileage from Reading on 4 occasions:	9	18	0
Bailiff 4 days at 17/6	3	10	0
Enquiry fee re. car:	1	1	0
	£20	19	0

I shall be obliged if you will please let me have your remittance
for this amount, otherwise I am instructed to remove your goods
for sale, without further delay.'

De profundis I wrote once more to Declan:

'Here is a copy of another letter received today from the Sheriff
of Berks. As you will see it now demands the immediate payment of £21 – or else. I haven't got it. I shall have to try and
borrow. Another day wasted. I am sick unto death of everything.
And you don't even bother to answer letters. I am sending a copy
of this to Babington-Smith.'

Another week went by and every day I expected the bailiffs,
the police, the auctioneer, and the pantechnicon, to be followed
by my ignominious eviction into the lane. Perhaps if I refused to
leave they would fire my thatch as the landlords used to do in
Ireland. Then on September 29, almost a month since the beginning of my persecution, during which time I had succeeded in
doing no work at all, came the following letter:

'My dear Peter,
    'This is to confirm that I have made payments in complete and
final settlement of the solicitor's demands. This is only what is
due to you and would have been done sooner if it had been in

my power to do so. But your remark and its implications, that I haven't bothered to answer your letters, I cannot just ignore. I have answered every letter you wrote and if there has been a day's delay it was because I was resorting to means to obtain your discharge from liability which I would never have resorted to for my own sake. Hope you are well.

Yours,

Declan.

'p.s. The only charges now unpaid are those of your local Sheriff's bums which my solicitor must challenge because they are excessive and incurred by the other side after I made the offer which was accepted.'

Suddenly I felt an unbelievable sense of relief; so much so that quite unwittingly I found myself once more loving Declan like a brother – or perhaps more like a brother-in-law. I went over to Aldbourne and told Jimmy Bomford the whole story. He lent me £20 and I paid off the Sheriff's charges. I then went home and went back to work on *Hadrian*.

A month passed and then one evening I wrote the word 'CURTAIN' at the foot of a page. *Hadrian* was finished – at least until its producer-to-be had seen it. Although I was too close to the subject to be very objective, I nevertheless thought that the play was promising. It had a good enough – perhaps even very good – leading part which might attract an actor of quality. Moreover, the Vatican Council was now in session and even the irreligious English were reading about Pope John in the newspapers. Personally I did not see how it could fail as a commercial enterprise. I said as much to my agent in a letter.

So there it was: 'CURTAIN'. I got up from the typewriter, took a thumb-stick from the porch, and went out. Summer had changed to autumn and the wheat and barley fields had long since been harvested and ploughed up. The sun was going down behind Marridge Hill as I walked towards it. A little way away a hare sat up, silhouetted against the fading light. At my approach it lolloped, prick-eared, slowly up hill as if it were hobbled by its too-long hind legs. Then in the manner of its kind it suddenly took fright, jinked left, put its ears back and flattened its belly to

218

the earth. Only then did it show what those hind legs were really for.

Further on was another wide field, newly ploughed, with spikes of yellow stubble sticking out of the purple furrows. A flock of lapwings got up as I came and flapped aimlessly about uttering their 'peewit' cries. Then, as I passed, they resettled one by one on the brown ploughed earth and stood facing into the wind.

Light was fading fast as I came down through Wiltshire Bottom. In the distance I saw a woman come out of Pitt Cottage and throw a plate of potato-peelings to some hens. A black and white dog with a teapot-handle tail followed and barked at someone, or something, in the direction of Lyckweed Farm.

I turned back along the crest of the hill and, as I reached home, the evening breeze stirred the tree-tops and the big elm gave out a gentle sigh.

EPILOGUE

At the time of writing this epilogue it must be fairly well known, at least to people who read or go to the theatre, that the play of *Hadrian the Seventh* became an outstanding success. In show business terms it was a smash hit, a box-office sell-out, and *Variety*, the American gospel of show business, headlined it as far as I can remember, 'H. VII; B-O, SOCKO!' The play to date has played in London, New York, Paris, Dublin, Vienna and Hamburg. It has played in Canada and the North American Continent, Mexico, the Argentine, Spain, Italy, Poland and Jugoslavia, and in Belgium, Holland, Sweden. It has played in Australia, in Rhodesia and in South Africa.[1] It has also been published in at least four different languages and translated into many more. Whatever I write about it from now on, therefore, can only be with hindsight. So what I now know is that *Hadrian the Seventh* is not a great play, but it certainly is a very good one; and one that is not dependent on a leading actor since it has been performed in so many countries with so many actors, each one of whom has been given the sole credit for its success.

The play of *Hadrian the Seventh* is an adaptation in the sense that it is based on Rolfe's book of the same title. The book is dramatic enough in itself but I knew when I sat down at Ragnals in my room, ten feet by seven feet, to make a play of it that I wanted to do more than just adapt. Frederick Rolfe, the self-styled Baron Corvo, had always written *romans à clefs* with himself as the ill-disguised hero. In this he played into my hands since it was easy

---

[1] There are two alternatives acceptable to the Writers Guild of Great Britain, to which I belong, in regard to performances of plays before segregated audiences. The first is to boycott: in other words to refuse to have one's work performed in front of a segregated audience. The second, is to permit the work to be performed, but to donate all royalties issuing therefrom to charity. I chose the latter course because it seemed the more positive way of going about things. Accordingly I donated my receipts to African charities under the auspices of the Archbishop of Pretoria.

enough to substitute Frederick William Rolfe for George Arthur Rose as the main protagonist. Having done so, it then became obvious that I should make the play a biography of Rolfe himself in terms of his 'Hadrian' fantasy. Having decided on this policy, I then set about reading everything by, or about, my subject that had ever been written, and in this I was helped by Mr Cecil Woolf who introduced me to material both published and unpublished that was at the time unknown to me. I should make it known at this point that at no time did I use the admirable biography *The Quest for Corvo* by A. J. Symons except as a bibliography.

In the course of my research I came across a number of contrary opinions about Rolfe's vocation for the priesthood. For example, a certain Canon Carmont, who had been a fellow student of Rolfe's at the Scots College in Rome, said, 'If Rolfe had any vocation for the priesthood, he certainly had none for the missionary work of the Scottish province, and he would have proved an encumbrance and a nuisance, at best'; so Canon Carmont continues smugly, 'we put our ideas regarding him before the Rector, and the Rector expelled him.' On the other hand another priest and a poet, Father Vincent O'Sullivan, said that, 'He was born for the Church; that was his main interest, and if the Catholics had kept him a priest he would have done them credit. . . .'

The more I read the more I became convinced that Father O'Sullivan was right and Canon Carmont wrong. Of course I would not for a moment like to suggest that I thought the author of the *Venice Letters* would have made a good parish priest. But I feel that the English Hierarchy of Rolfe's day were so deeply imbued by the Victorian – and therefore Anglican – *mores* of the period that they were incapable of having a catholic [*sic*] approach to a problem which might have enabled them to give him the priesthood. Had they done so Rolfe would never have gone to Venice and would therefore not have committed to paper some of the most eloquent essays in homosexual pornography ever written. My own private view at the time of writing the play was, therefore, quite the opposite to that of Carmont: I felt that Rolfe was admirably suited by temperament to have become a missionary in, let us say, an African leper-colony, or some such institution where his energy and imperviousness to hardship would have enabled him to pursue his vocation in the eyes of God and to serve a useful purpose for the benefit of man. But then of course we would not have had his books.

These then were the sum of my thoughts and feelings when, in the spring of 1961, I went down to Ragnals Cottage to set about my solitary task of writing a play about this solitary man. When I had finished the first draft in the early autumn of the same year my experience of having been on the production side of a drama programme convinced me that I had hold of something good. This faith kept me buoyant in subsequent months so that I plagued my agent, Harvey Unna, at every significant moment: for example, at the time of the Ecumenical Council in Rome; at the time of Pope John XXIII's death; at the time of Pope Paul's election, each time urging him to take advantage of what seemed to be a new interest in the affairs of the Church of Rome.

It was all to no avail, though small blame to Harvey. Everybody for one reason or another was frightened of it. Of the impresarios, those orientated towards the Anglican Church feared that it would offend Catholics and those who were Jewish feared that it would offend Christians of all denominations. Of the number of prominent actors approached, those who were Catholic regarded the play as being anti-Catholic, and those who were Protestant thought it was pro-Catholic propaganda. No one would touch it and I gave up hope. If I hadn't by this time quite lost interest in the whole thing, thereby ceasing to think about it at all, I would undoubtedly have been forced to the conclusion that I had written a dud.

Of course, when anybody from time to time showed any interest, I sat up and took notice. It is a fact of life that every impresario, every director, every leading actor in the game feels that they have something to contribute to a writer's script. Very often they have, and equally often they have not. But I went along with all but the most absurd suggestions that were made, making as far as possible good use of the best of them. The final script has now been published.[1] I have also in my possession the

[1] André Deutsch, 1968. Alfred Knopf, 1969. Penguin, 1969.

first draft incorporating many excellent suggestions made by Jimmie Roose-Evans and curiously this draft is in essence much the same as the final published version. At some future date, if anyone were to think it worth while, a comparison might be interesting. But, as I say, after about five years in the wilderness I had lost interest in *Hadrian the Seventh*, and naturally enough I was quite occupied doing other things.

Then in 1966 a friend of mine, the talented director Charles Jarrott, said: 'I've found an Angel. Got anything up your sleeve?'

'No,' I said, 'only that old Pope thing.'

'Let's have a read of it then,' said Charles.

I gave him the script and forgot all about it again.

Some weeks, or maybe months, later Charles rang me up.

'They want to do it,' he said.

'Do it?'

'Yes.'

'Do what?'

'Your play, you silly bastard.'

'Oh,' I said, being genuinely confused. I had around this time been writing television plays for the BBC. My confusion must have conveyed itself to Charles.

'I don't think you know what the hell I am talking about. You wrote a stage play called *Hadrian the Seventh*. Remember?'

To cut a long story short, Charles soon afterwards introduced me to two nice men: one a short Canadian and the other a tall American. They were very agreeable to me and did not require more than their statutory two-penn'orth of alterations to the text. So the play was duly produced at the Birmingham Repertory Theatre in May 1967 – a mere six years after it had first been written. The irony of it was that Charles Jarrott, who had 'discovered' it, was never able to direct it owing to an offer of an important film which he would have been a fool to turn down. Instead *Hadrian* was produced by the Birmingham Rep's resident director, Peter Dews, who was at that time – though is no longer – an old enemy of mine.

However, despite Dews's very able production, and despite a laudatory notice by J. C. Frewin, the critic, who had been a strong champion of the play from its inception, *Hadrian* was a flop. Apart from a handful of curious priests from nearby Oscott College, Rolfe's first seminary, none of the citizens of Brumagem bothered to come. They were saving up their brass for a revival of *Charlie's Aunt*.

The last time I went to see the production was on a Saturday matinée when, by kind permission of the Theatre management, Old Age Pensioners were allowed in for a nominal fee. And there they sat, the Old Age Pensioners, a mere handful of them, scattered here and there about the stalls, soporific after their midday meal, belching, farting and snoring all the way through Alec McCowen's exquisite performance. Then, and only then, did I believe the play to be a total failure.

When a whole year later the same two impresarios, Bill Freedman and Charles Kasher, put the play on at the Mermaid Theatre, London, I was in a remote village in southern Spain where I had been directing a film for the BBC. Not even when a number of mutilated, but seemingly optimistic, telegrams began filtering through to the bar in which I had made my headquarters did I think for a moment that it was going to be a case of Ragnals to riches.

Spero meliora!